THE TIGER HUNTERS

By the same Author

SPORT AND WILD LIFE IN THE DECCAN
A BOOK OF MAN-EATERS
THE BOOK OF THE TIGER
THE HISTORY OF THE HYDERABAD CONTINGENT
WELLINGTON'S CAMPAIGNS IN INDIA
NAPOLEON'S CAMPAIGNS IN ITALY
FROM BOULOGNE TO AUSTERLITZ
NAPOLEON'S INVASION OF RUSSIA
Etc.

THE SUBADAR.
Descendant of Soldiers of Fortune.

THE TIGER HUNTERS

BRIGADIER-GENERAL R.G. BURTON

"Our Youth is like the Dream of the Hunter on the Hill of Heath." —OSSIAN

With illustrations

MITTAL PUBLICATIONS
NEW DELHI-110059 [INDIA]

Photographically reproduced from 1936 edition entitled "*The Tiger Hunter*"

2002

Editorial Office:
 H-13, Bali Nagar,
 New Delhi - 110015
 Phones: 5163610, 5431361

Showroom:
 4594/9, Daryaganj,
 New Delhi - 110002
 Phone: 3250398

Published and printed by Naurang Rai for Mittal Publications, A-110, Mohan Garden, New Delhi-110059, India.
Tel.: 5351493, 5357128 *Telefax:* 91-11-5351521
E-Mail : mittalp@ndf.vsnl.net.in   *Gram* : Mittalbux
website : www.mittalpublications.com

CONTENTS

PROLOGUE

The Dream of the Hunter 17
Mount Pisgah—Rivers in flood—The Old Cantonment—The lakes—Wildfowl—Thugs—Lakshmi the elephant—The children—Birds in the banyan tree—Pale phantoms of the past—Carissima—Native attendants—The ayah—The ruling race—Troopers—Wazir Khan—Shaikh Karim—Nathu shikari—The distant hills—Servitors—The bungalow—Flying foxes—Night—The morning ride—Parade and manœuvres—My uniform—Active service—Boot and saddle—The last expedition—The morning march—Roadside scenes—Farewell—Desolation—Bijli the camel—A day's sport—Great Bustard—Antelope and sandgrouse—Partridges—Blackbuck—Jungle and field—In the shadow of the trees—The Persian wheel—Wild animals at water—Homeward—A scene of sorrow—Death of a hero—The fight in the fort—The Last Post.

CHAPTER I

The House by the Stream 34
India and England—Indian villages—Indian animals—Game birds—East and West—English scenes—Indian birds—The house—Time stays, we go—Morning prayers—The silver thread—Fish and dams—Tickling trout—Progress—Fresh interests—Education—The heritage of the sword—Nature—Birds and their nests—Lepidoptera—Literary tastes.

CHAPTER II

The School near the Sea 45
The school—The murmur of the waves—Ruins on the hill—The whelming tide—The promontory—Wrecks and wreckers—Dead sailor—School life—The sea

passage—School food—Bathing in the nude—More food—Varied sport—Sea-fishing—Bird-hunting—Birds' nests—Jackdaws' cave—Fights in the ring—The Victorian Age—Victorian women—The spirit of adventure—England and Englishmen—Work in distant lands—School learning—A notable French master—The obsequies of Napoleon—Leaving school.

CHAPTER III

WEST INDIAN EPISODE 56
Voyage to Jamaica—The sailors of Columbus—Sea wolves—St. Thomas—Haiti and San Domingo—Pirates—Tortuga—Voodoo drums—Jamaica—Fort Augusta—The Palisadoes—Kingston—West India Regiment—Mutiny in Trinidad—Daaga the Chief—Military execution—Port Royal—Henry Morgan—Soldiers—Fauna of Jamaica—Sharks and sailors—Enteric fever—Yellow Jack—The distant land—Barbados—Jane Ann—A midshipman's wraith—Bridgetown—Murder in court—The murderer's ordeal—Restless grave of Christchurch—Wonders of the deep—Sport on the island—The far horizon.

CHAPTER IV

FOREST AND MOUNTAIN 73
Wild men and wild beasts—Antelope and gazelle—Cantonment life—Tiger kills an officer—The hunter's death—The assassin's bullet—Thugs—Dacoits—Tantia Bhil—The India of my dreams—Ride to the forest—A tiger in the way—Bears and bison—Encounter with a tigress—Aggressive bears—Porcupines—A wayside panther—Panther and bear in camp—Bison killed—A great bear—Wild dogs—Wild animals at water—Monkeys' antics—Panther and monkeys—Four-horned antelope—Tiger kills bison and vulture—Mountain passes—Rock-hewn shrines—Buried treasure—Rebels in the forest—Sport in the plains—Hunting leopards—Migratory birds—Florican.

CHAPTER V

THE OLD CANTONMENT 85
Return journey—View from the hill—Deserted cantonments—Famine in the land—Famine relief—Wild life

CONTENTS 9

in drought—Small game—Great bustard—Digging out
a panther—Banjaras—Chief killed by a panther—
Preparations for expedition—Tents—Rifles and guns—
Monkeys in the compound—A cobra killed—The heat
of the day—Baggage and stores—Camp followers.

CHAPTER VI

INTO THE WILDS 97
An early start—The Subadar—Generations of soldiers
—A 40-mile ride—Antelope—Under the banyan tree—
The field of Assaye—Relics of the past—Pindaris—
Thugs—Murdered travellers—An old fort—Days of
long ago—The jungle path—A tigress passes by—
Effects of drought—The dead wayfarer—Relief and
irrigation—The valley and the river—Arrival in camp
—The shikaris.

CHAPTER VII

THE SHRINE ON THE HILL 109
Morning in camp—The way through the jungle—The
Valley of Shaikh Farid—The shrine on the hill—
Sacrifice at the ziarat—Jungle scenery—Wild beasts in
cover—Dangerous bees—Tracks of tigress—Picketed
calves—Gazelles—A brave herdsman—The panther's
call—Buckshot cartridges—A man-eating panther—
Panthers or leopards—The cheetah.

CHAPTER VIII

THE FIRST TIGER HUNT 119
Up with the sun—Kill by tigress—The beat in Shaikh
Farid kora—Peacocks and stag—I wound the tigress—
A panther passes—Following the tigress—Nathu faces
the tigress—The tigress killed—Whiskers for poison—
Chichkora and tracks—The jungle god—Goat sacrificed
—The Spirit of the Wild—Human sacrifice—Reception
of tigress—Skinning the tigress—Lucky bones and fat
—The wild and the free.

CHAPTER IX

VOICES IN THE FOREST 131
Birds and beasts—Voices by day and night—The bird
of dawn—Under the stars—Notes of alarm—Monkeys

and peafowl—The charm of the jungle—Teeming animal life—False morning—The forest over the river—Four-horned antelope—A kill in a tree—Game on the hillside—Stag shot—Picketing buffaloes—Events in Chichkora—Robert kills the tiger—Tigress and cubs—Spear thrown at boar—Nilgai—Another tiger shot—The tiger's kill—Tigers and porcupines—Worm in tiger's eye.

CHAPTER X

A MIXED BAG 146

Storm in the hills—Tigress and cubs depart—Shooting peafowl—Under the mohwa tree—Valuable blossoms—Great vitality of blue bull—Bear and ant hill—The Flame of the Forest—Sloth bear—A sounder of pig—Boar killed—Kill by a panther—Vigil by night—Death of the panther—Buckshot cartridges.

CHAPTER XI

THE EMPIRE OF NATURE 156

Wandering tigers—Forward plans—Bears on the hills—Banjaras—Bear and cub killed—Two more bears shot—Tracking the wounded—Migration of the tiger—A kill in the forest—Nathu and the tiger—Death of the tiger—Tigers and cattle—Sylvan solitudes—Nathu and Bhima—Crocodiles—A funeral pyre—Turtles devour a corpse—A Sikh colony.

CHAPTER XII

DESTROYERS IN THE FOREST 167

Death for ever at work—Tigers—Panthers—Bears—Hyena—Cheetah—Wild dog—Wolves—Smaller cats and vermin—A pool in the moonlight—The tiger's skeleton—The buffalo at the pool—The tiger slays—Flight of the tiger—Bull bison kills a buffalo—History of the night—Bison—Tiger eats crabs and snake—Blue bull—Moving camp—Scene on the river—Malabar squirrels—Imperial pigeon—Kill by a panther—Balance of Nature—Survival of the fittest—The hills of Ambari—Kill by a tigress—The tigress shot—A bear passes by—Stag shot—Uses of deer-skin—Scene in forest glade—Wild dog killed.

CONTENTS

CHAPTER XIII

THE GREAT AMBARI TIGER 177
Ambari—Camp at Ganeshpur—The tigers of Ambari—
Tigers in water—Thunderstorm—The tiger passes by
—The great Ambari tiger—Jadu or sorcery—The
jungle god—Unsuccessful beat—A long day's hunt—
The cook put to flight—The tiger escapes again—The
kill in the water—Sunstroke—The tiger tracked down
—Countryside gather to the beat—The beaters—The
tiger hemmed in—Attempted escape frustrated—
Death of the great tiger—Length of tigers—Mighty
hunters—Robert stalks a tigress—Hunting by scent
or sight ?

CHAPTER XIV

THE MONARCH OF THE GLEN 193
A march eastwards—The great banyan tree—Birds in
the tree—Wild dogs shot—A Banjara chief—The new
encampment—Exploration of valley and ravine—A
tiger near camp—The tiger escapes—Timid tigers—
Another bear shot—Fish eats snake—An elusive tiger—
The tiger tracked down—Death of the tiger—The tiger's
lair—Two tigers shot.

CHAPTER XV

SAFETY LAST ! 203
A wounded tiger—Panther killed—Nathu belabours a
panther—Following the tiger—A near thing—Death
of the tiger—Tigress and cubs—Cobra speared—
·Poachers—The medicine man—Three panthers shot—
Scaly anteater—The verge of the unknown—A fierce
tigress—The country of the Gonds.

CHAPTER XVI

ABORIGINAL GONDS 213
Character of aborigines—Variation—Habits—Scarcity
—Jungle produce—Gond gods—The Great Spirit—
Sufferings of Gonds and Korkus—The River of Blood
—Kali, the Dark goddess—A fearful rite—A splendid
country—The Indian bison—The man-eater—The
victim's spirit—Indru, that great Hunter—Through
the great forest—The lake and fort—The Raja's visit

—The visit returned—Panther eats a boy—Sport on the lake—Crocodiles—Wild duck—Fishing—Flooded out—Deserted temples.

CHAPTER XVII

THE EMPIRE OF NIGHT 227
Sounds that live in darkness—A tigress killed—A tigress escapes—Building a machan—A vigil by night—Spotted deer—Monkeys—Mongoose—The lake by night—Hyena visits the kill—Invisible tigress—Shooting in the dark—An angry tiger—The tiger killed—Obliterative colouration—Moving on—Crossing the plateau—A gloomy glen—Camp in the wilds—Queer fish—Cyclonic storm—Two tigers shot—Noisy animals—How they hunt—Tiger killed—Two tigresses escape—Death of a Rohilla—Rumours of a man-eater.

CHAPTER XVIII

TRACKS OF DEATH 240
A man-eating panther—Tracks of famine—Wayside graves—Causes of man-eating—Panther and bees—Panther killed with buckshot—Man-eating tiger—Death of the man-eater—The man-eater's "leavings"—Heads, feet, and hands—Murder by thugs.

LIST OF ILLUSTRATIONS

The Subadar	*Frontispiece*
	FACING PAGE
The Bungalow	22
The School by the Sea	23
Pitiless Rocks	58
Men of the First West India Regiment	59
Barbados	74
The Old Mess-House	75
The Cheetah Hunt	120
The Winding River	121
Chandru and Nathu, Shikaris	158
A Tiger in the Beat	159
The Tiger Slain	200
Vultures	201
Camp in the Forest	232
Small Game	233
Trophies of the Chase	233

FOREWORD

How much of this story is fact, and how much is fancy? Certainly there is in the early part some of "the stuff that dreams are made on," but even where a dream-child haunts these pages, imagination and reality are closely interwoven and every incident is an episode of actual life within the knowledge or the experience of the writer. While some liberties have been taken in relation to time and persons, all activities herein described have been arranged in narrative form in order to give cohesion to a tale of adventure which would otherwise have to be divided into disconnected periods.

The pursuit of big game and all connected with it has been lived through in every detail by the author in person, sometimes as a solitary hunter and at others in company with a much-loved brother who has long since passed through the gates of war to the Happy Hunting Grounds, where we may hope to meet again. And throughout adventurous years there have been with me those Indian friends, comrades, and faithful followers, most of whom have gone forever from this world, whose memory cannot be recalled without a pang of regret that we shall never meet again in life. To them, the gallant Subadar, the brave shikaris, and all the others, living or dead, the hunter owes a debt of gratitude for valuable service, and dedicates this book.

R.G.B.

THE TIGER HUNTERS

PROLOGUE

THE DREAM OF THE HUNTER

THE height we called Mount Pisgah, from afar off so like a barren northern fell, on whose summit I often and through many years indulged in day dreams, overlooked from a distance of two or three miles the old cantonment where I first saw the light. To this place a road wound for nearly a hundred miles from the main highway running North and South through the centre of peninsular India, passing over hill and plain, arable and jungle land, across streams and dry watercourses which became rivers during the rainy season. On either side of such rivers stood a small bungalow or rest-house for travellers to shelter in until the flood subsided after a heavy fall of rain, sometimes a matter of twenty-four hours or more, for there were no bridges and the mail bags had to be passed over the stream by means of ropes and pulleys.

Our cantonment was much like other remote military stations of those days, garrisoned only by native troops. There were thatched bungalows inhabited by the English officers, each house with white walls standing in its own compound surrounded by few or many trees—pipal, mango, palm, acacia, and tamarind, and sometimes a giant banyan tree. Beyond the bungalows were the mud-built "lines" of the native troops, cavalry, infantry, and a battery of artillery whose smooth-bore guns throwing a nine-pound shot were drawn by bullocks, while beyond these lines the bazaar, consisting chiefly of squalid mud huts but with a few good houses of the wealthier inhabitants, had grown up round the old native village and had gradually spread and prospered from the profits of supplying the wants of the troops. Here were small shops chiefly for the sale of grain and pulse, clarified butter, sweetmeats, fruit, and vegetables, as well as the workshops of the artificers in silver, brass, and leather. But otherwise there had been little change during the many years that had elapsed since the first occupation of the cantonment.

The military station had been established to pacify the country and keep order in a region where thugs, Pindaris, and other robbers had from early times committed depredations, such as still broke out occasionally among elements who viewed with dismay and opposed with force the growth of effective power in the land where they had for so long carried on with impunity their lawless mode of life.

On the far side of the bazaar a watercourse, called the river, was in the hot weather so far dried up by the heat of the sun that the stream stopped flowing, and holes had to be dug in the sandy bed to get water percolating into these shallow and improvised wells. But the outstanding features of the cantonment were the two artificial lakes, called tanks, made by damming watercourses with anicuts or embankments now thickly grown with ancient trees, the largest covering many acres during the rainy season; this sheet of water was beyond the southern border of the place, remote from all buildings, while the bazaar clustered on the bank of the smaller tank. In the cold season there was good sport to be had when duck, snipe, and other wildfowl, including geese, grey cranes, spoonbills, and flamingoes, flocked to the reedy banks. But often in the height of summer the great lake was almost dry, when fish used to take refuge in the mud at the bottom and there lie dormant until the welcome rains beginning at the end of June brought them and all living things much-needed relief.

It was in a dry ravine or tributary of the watercourse that a number of bodies of people murdered by thugs were disinterred close to the cantonment and the road. These were the victims of a band of stranglers whose leader was a respectable merchant of the place; many were killed in the bazaar by this man and his myrmidons, among other victims a wealthy inhabitant of a distant town, together with his servants and other attendants, the merchandise he was travelling with being openly sold in the bazaar by the leader of the thugs.

My first recollection is of sitting on a bright-coloured Persian rug under Lakshmi Hathi's trunk with the children from the nearby bungalow in the shade of the great wide-branching banyan tree whose tendrils hung down on every side. Lakshmi was my father's elephant. She would swing her trunk to and fro over us, wielding a horse-tail whisk with a silver handle to keep the flies off us. There we would sit and play, safe under the protection of the great elephant for hours at a time. We had wooden and clay toys from the bazaar—elephants, tigers, panthers, bears, bison, deer, and antelope—and we would make believe that we were hunting in the jungle; the rug had on it coloured patterns of jungle landscapes and animals to work in with our schemes. Always in the hunt I would want to shoot the tigers and would pay little attention to most other beasts, although panthers and leopards, bears, and bison were not to be despised.

The banyan tree swarmed with birds; there was the little green coppersmith or barbet with its sharp metallic note; the green pigeons with their delicate mauve neck feathers and their soft whistle like that of a schoolboy, so unlike the cooing of other doves; bright emerald green flycatchers having long beaks and flying every now and then from the tree and returning to their perches with the prize, and bulbuls displaying scarlet patches behind. In the hot weather the koel of the cuckoo tribe, known as the brain-fever bird, shrieked from the topmost branches with an ever-increasing crescendo of notes until we thought it would burst, especially when we imitated it and excited it to more frequent repetition of its call; and the noisy little owls quarrelled in the dusk at sunset, while the great owl hooted from a distant perch. Lizards and palm-squirrels racing up and down and round the tree, and squeaking about the verandah, helped to keep us amused.

But this was long before the time of which I write, for I was now a well-grown boy of eleven and my playing at hunting wild animals had already become a reality so far as the antelope were concerned, although I had not as yet met with beasts more dangerous than wolves that would make off at sight, and hyenas shambling furtively across the plain at early dawn. The other children had gone long ago; some had faded away and one by one crept silently to rest where they were laid forever in the little graves marked by white stones under the dark cypresses within the four stone walls of the cemetery by the palm-fringed lake; others had sailed across the sea to that far distant England of which I had heard so much but had never seen. My mother too, a half-remembered vision of early years, lay there in the graveyard where so many of my little companions, pale phantoms of the past, here to-day and gone to-morrow, were forever silent. Sometimes at night I seemed to hear the little pattering feet and shrill voices of the children of long ago, echoing once more in the compound or in the verandah; and then, when the heat was too great for sleep, my mother's blue eyes would look at me lovingly out of the gloom of the tropical night where I lay under the mosquito curtain, and I would see her hair shining like spun gold in the light of the moon.

I used to go with my father every Sunday to lay flowers on her grave, marked by a broken column with the single word "Carissima" engraved in the stone. She had suddenly disappeared from my life more than five years before the time of which I write, and since then the only woman I remember was Ayah, my faithful and devoted attendant, ever ready to sacrifice herself to my slightest whim. The young master in the East is apt to be very exacting, so she must have had a somewhat trying life. There were of course others, very few in that small and remote cantonment, wives of my father's brother-officers who came and went, but only Ayah took the place of my mother in caring for me. She was still there, even now when I was growing big, and she looked after my clothes and waited on me hand and foot, a devoted and patient slave.

Then there were many male attendants, all my faithful servitors, tyrannised over, I fear, at times but ever ready to do my bidding, with whom, while holding despotic sway, I was on the friendliest terms, although I allowed no familiarity. In those days and long afterwards the prestige and predominance of the ruling race was taken for granted and extended even to the very young. All men of colour bowed down at the feet of the Baba Sahib; even the native officers and troopers who used to ride into the compound on duty with my father, who was commandant of the irregular cavalry regiment, or who were on guard at the gate of the commandant's house in accordance with old and long-established custom, would salaam to me as to an officer, for I was not only the colonel's son but had myself been with the regiment during the whole of my short life

Old Wazir Khan, the butler, had served my father since his arrival in India some thirty years before this time; he was a grave and reverend Moslem with a long white beard down to his waist, proud of the fair complexion and blue eyes that told of his Rohilla descent, and dressed always in spotless white. His little son, Abdul, of my own age and almost as fair as myself, was one of my early playfellows. I call Wazir Khan old, yet he cannot have been more than forty-five, for he entered my father's service as a boy to wait at table, a post now held by Abdul, who always stood behind my chair.

Then there was Yakub Khan, a duffadar or sergeant, batman and general factotum, who had carried me about as a baby and had taught me to ride and shoot at the target. Another faithful friend was Nathu, shikari, looking old at forty, but active and untiring, who had been with my father at the death of a hundred tigers, many of whose striped skins adorned the walls and floor of our bungalow. He was lean and spare, as hard as a gnarled tree trunk to which his mahogany-coloured face, pulled on one side by a panther's claws, bore much resemblance. He always carried an eight-foot spear when out in the fields and jungle, and his whole

THE BUNGALOW.
A long, thatched building, with a deep and wide verandah.

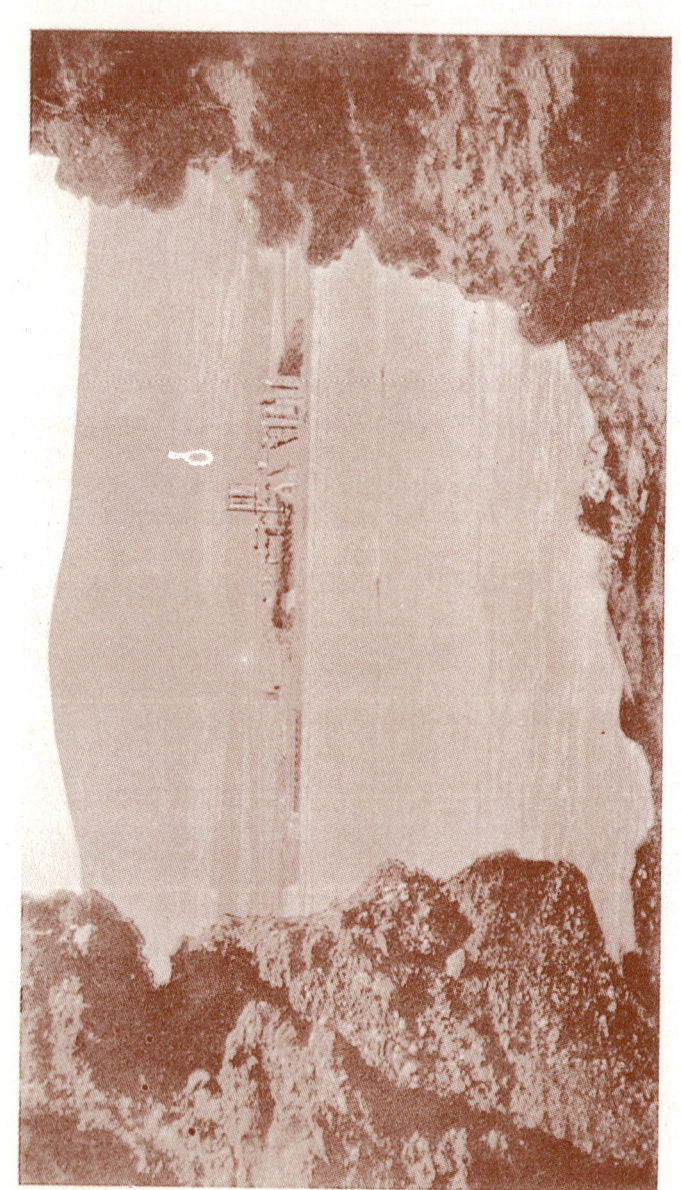

THE SCHOOL.

Facing the sea, four-square to all the winds that blow.

talk was of wild beasts, their habits, and his adventures in hunting them in my father's company. But he despised all except the tiger, for whom he had a wholesome respect; even the panther that had wounded him he regarded with contempt as scarcely worthy of notice. " Panthers ! " he would exclaim, " they are only wild cats and of little account ! " I always said that I would hunt tigers when I grew up, and Nathu would wag his scarred head with approval and promise that he would go with me and show me many tigers. And then he would launch out into a description of the jungles beyond the far horizon, pointing to the valleys and rivers and the range of hills dimly outlined in the distance on a clear day and forming the longed-for goal of my ambition.

Besides the servitors and attendants and others already mentioned there was the mahout who had his charge Lakshmi at a word; I would help him to feed the elephant with great piles of chupathis, flat unleavened cakes made of flour like huge pancakes. And there was a whole host of lesser servants about the house and compound—water-carriers, horse-keepers, dog-boys, and all the vast establishment that went to make up the numerous suite of a colonel of the Indian Army in olden days.

Our bungalow was a long low thatched building with many doors that were never shut except in the heat of the day and the height of the hot weather, when they were for the most part blocked with frames filled with sweet-smelling kuskus grass, over which water was thrown to keep the house cool; a deep and wide verandah ran round three sides of the house. There was an upper storey containing two bedrooms where my father and I slept, and an open platform on the roof, surrounded by a low parapet, where my bed stood in the hot weather under the starry canopy of the sky when the stifling atmosphere precluded sleep indoors. Here we could hope to catch the fugitive breeze, although when that came it was often like a breath from Hades and gave little relief from the burning heat. There I used sometimes to lie awake for hours in the night, looking up at the stars and listening to the gathered cry of jackals which began to yell soon after the flying foxes, those great fruit bats, had passed overhead on their nightly flight to feed on the figs in the giant banyan trees. Towards dawn the air would sometimes blow fresh and cool, and then I would sleep until the sun was on the point of rising. I would jump out of bed, splash for a few minutes in the bath, dress hastily in white riding breeches and shirt, pull on my brown boots made of soft deer-skin, and with a sun-hat on my head ride forth on my grey Arab pony, accompanied by Yakub Khan or sometimes with one of the native officers or troopers on the mornings when my father was occupied with his regiment. Sometimes I would ride with him on parade during morning drill or field manœuvres; and on grand occasions, when there was a ceremonial parade, I would wear the dress of the regiment—a dark green long coat or kaftan with scarlet facings, trimmed with gold lace, scarlet waist sash, leather belt, white breeches, and black knee boots, and a lungi or turban with hanging ends of green and gold.

The regiment was sometimes called out on active service at a few hours' notice in those turbulent times when the country was still infested by bands of armed robbers. Then I was left in charge of Yakub Khan, while at night the house was protected by the guard of troopers mounted at the gate where a tent was pitched for them. And so I grew up with

PROLOGUE

the sound of the trumpet constantly in my ears, used to association with troops, and often seeing my father ride off at the head of the regiment an hour after the call to "boot and saddle," to hunt down marauders or perhaps to carry by assault a stronghold fifty miles off held by desperate men.

I shall never forget the last time when my father rode out on the expedition from which he never returned alive. The regiment moved off at daybreak, as I had often seen them start with my father at their head. They rode forth with flying pennons on their lances, sabres at their sides, and carbines at the saddle-bow, followed by gaily-caparisoned camels carrying the bell-mouthed camel-guns mounted on and fired from the back of the animal. They were a brave sight, the troopers riding on red-quilted saddles known as kogirs, with reins of twisted red and white cotton rope. They rode forth as they had so often done, to attack a body of marauders who had taken up a position in a mud and stone fort near a village about fifty miles off, from which they had issued to harry the country and plunder the neighbouring habitations.

Mounted on my Arab pony, I accompanied my father for about three or four miles, and every incident and scene on the road, a mere cattle-track across country, on that last ride is stamped on my memory for ever. It was early January; the sun had not risen when we started, and the morning air struck chill upon me; dawn was coming and in the east the sky was all pink like the wing of a flamingo. The bright dewdrops were like frost upon the grass until they faded away under the rays of the risen sun, and as we rode along we heard the grey partridges calling by the roadside and the painted francolin whose harsh and grating call: "Shaikh

Farid! Shaikh Farid!" resounded from tall elephant grass and scanty bush, from which at times they rose on whirring wings. A herd of antelope, led by a fine black buck whose spiral horns lay along his back, galloped across the road in front of us and stood at gaze within a hundred yards before continuing their flight with astounding high bounds in the air at starting; and a striped hyena, foul scavenger of the night, shadowy grey in the dim morning light, lobbed off with slouching gait across the fields to his den in the stony-hearted hills.

I rode beside my father for some miles on the way at the head of the regiment and then said "Good-bye!" and after the squadrons had all passed me with many greetings, I turned back with my escort of Yakub Khan and a trooper. Something seemed to chill me with a foreboding of evil. I was used to seeing my father off, but on this morning as I turned back to ride home I felt a strange sense of desolation; I seemed to be all alone in the world, although I loved my life amid these wild surroundings, so remote from the busy life of cities which I have always hated. My Arab pony pecked at the point where we entered the cantonment, but I pulled him up and rode into the compound, dismounted, and left him with the groom, and went to see Lakshmi Hathi have her food, a mountain of chupathis. I then ran to the house where Wazir Khan salaamed to me on the threshold, and Ayah came and told me my bath was ready, but still the sense of desolation oppressed me, as I remember now when looking back through so many long years; I was so lonely and I had an almost unconscious foreboding that my father had passed out of my life forever.

Next morning I had quite recovered my usual spirits. I went out with Nathu shikari soon after daybreak on Bijli (her name meaning " Lightning "), the swift-footed riding-camel, to hunt antelope and anything else we could find. Bijli was fitted with a double-seated saddle and would carry not only two people at a speed of six to nine miles an hour, but our rifle and guns and provisions for the day, while game could be slung across her back for the return journey. Nathu rode in front, guiding Bijli by the rope attached to a wooden peg for which her nose was pierced. At a word she would squat for me to dismount when a chance of a shot offered.

We stayed out all day; I shot a black buck with fine horns twenty-four inches long, and a wolf from a pair we found pulling in half and devouring a gazelle they had just killed; the other one raced away across country, while my second shot kicked up the dust behind it. We saw a great bustard with a white head, as big as a turkey, and we circled round and round it several times on camel-back, reducing the radius at each circuit, the only way to approach within range of this wary bird, but I did not get a shot and it flapped out of sight on ceaselessly beating wings. Then we took our shot-guns and added some sandgrouse and partridges to the bag. The sandgrouse used to afford excellent sport. We knew their drinking haunts at pools to which they resorted morning and evening, where I could almost set my watch by them, so punctual were they at the watering place. At about half-past eight we used to hide behind bushes within thirty yards of the water. Soon afterwards would be heard the distant cries announcing the first comers of the flight, and a few birds would appear on the far horizon, rapidly approaching with unerring instinct towards the pool. Sometimes they would alight at once close to the water or they might circle around overhead and offer difficult shots. Sometimes large packs would suddenly sweep overhead and settle motionless on the stony plain, where their colour and form assimilated so closely and wonderfully with the ground that they would disappear on the instant of alighting as though the earth had swallowed them up.

Partridges were more difficult to bag, especially the grey ones, for they would run and run, but sometimes crouch in the bushes where we could walk them up and shoot them as they rose. The painted francolin was the better bird. It did not run, but its persistent call would betray its presence in bush or grass clump, and when we approached it would rise straight up on whirring wings and offer a fine shot, as often missed as hit. It was a handsome bird with dark brown, beautifully mottled plumage, and more prized for the table than the grey one, which was something of a scavenger, frequenting the outskirts of the villages. Then there were green pigeons in the trees, and blue rocks in the sides of the deep wells and the dilapidated walls of old forts, and little quail in the fields of cotton and pulse.

The black buck was a fine fellow. He would walk proudly about with his herd of does, always showing restlessness as we came near on camel-back. Sometimes the herd would make to bolt, the animals springing several feet high in the air, and then the buck would prod the does behind with his horns to make them move and hurry up and be off. Or we might find a buck with one doe he had chosen and driven 'from the herd, or at some seasons four or five fine bucks would be seen by themselves separate from the herd of does and young.

On these long days I loved the sights and sounds of the jungle and the fields as much as the hunting and shooting. I liked to watch the husbandmen ploughing the fields with their bullocks, the plough such as had been in use from time immemorial, a mere log of wood shaped like a great blunt arrow to turn over the soil. It was said that when an iron plough had been introduced, the natives set it up at the end of a field instead of using it, and painted it red just as they paint great stones to represent the god of the jungle. It was a pleasure also to watch bullocks patiently drawing from a well with a Persian wheel the water that ran down the channels to irrigate fields and gardens of betel nut and sugar cane and bananas that surrounded the hamlets.

In times of drought the only water in the neighbourhood was to be found in the wells and channels near the villages. At night when all was quiet and the watchmen slumbered on their platforms amid the crops where they were posted to drive away wild animals with shouts or slings or wooden scares, the nilgai used to come down to drink where the water had collected, or at the wooden troughs, hollowed out of the trunks of trees, which were placed for the cattle near the wells. The marks of their feet could be plainly seen in the dust of the paths or in the soft damp mud every morning. At night, too, the prowling panther visited these drinking places, where he might find a victim among the herds of gazelle that trooped down in the dark from the neighbouring arid hills, or where he might pick up a stray goat or dog, or a calf that was perishing of thirst. The gazelles drank here in numbers, leaving a beaten pathway from their jungle haunts.

But generally we avoided the unsavoury surroundings of the villages, although I knew and talked in the fields with many of the simple-minded and friendly inhabitants who passed their lives of toil in happy and Arcadian contentment. At midday we would rest in the shade of fine trees, mango, or banyan, or pipal; the tamarind was to be avoided, except to gather some of the sharp and acrid fruit, because of the cattle ticks whose bite would cause fever and make the feet and ankles swell. Bijli would squat and Nathu would lift my basket down from the saddle when we had dismounted, and then while I had luncheon he would eat his own meal at a distance. And so the long day, never a moment too long on these expeditions, passed and we would trot home in the cool of the evening with Bijli at a speed of eight miles an hour.

This day the sun was getting low when Bijli's bells tinkled merrily as we rode swiftly homeward across the plain. From the high ground where we paused for a few minutes overlooking the cantonment in the valley below, we saw in the distance a trail of dust hanging on the evening air, marking the approach of the returning cavalry. Nathu pointed it out and said: "There baba sahib is your father coming back with the risala (regiment)"; and I replied that it was too far to make him out, although I could see the glint of steel spear-heads in the light of the setting sun. Then we trotted fast down the road from the hill, skirted the lake, entered the cantonment, and rode on towards the bungalow. Suddenly, as we approached, the sound of a great clamour struck upon our ears; we saw a throng of people pouring from the bazaars, and as we came to the gateway of our compound a sad scene, never to be effaced from my memory, came before our eyes.

How clearly it all rises before me now as I look back through the vista of many long years. There was a sound of weeping and wailing within, which I well knew from previous experience of the ways of these simple people marked the presence of death. A chill struck upon my heart. And then I saw a troop of cavalry dismounted, dust-covered, lining the road through the compound to the house. The Major of the regiment met me at the gate, and when the camel knelt he lifted me from the saddle and set me down. " What is the matter ? What has happened ? Where is Father ? " I cried, although I had a certain knowledge of disaster and knew in my heart that he was dead. The Major led me by the hand into the house, between the lines of troopers who stood with bent heads, many of whom I could see were moved to tears. Yakub Khan came forward, tears streaming down his cheeks. " Baba sahib ! Baba sahib ! " was all that he could say. Then old Wazir Khan came and bowed down and laid his turban at my feet and threw dust upon his head. And so I knew that my father was dead.

In the desolate house they had laid him in his uniform, just as he had died, his sabre at his side and his hand upon the hilt, and his blue scarlet-lined cloak laid across him. He looked very pale, but so calm and peaceful that he might have been asleep.

They told me how it had happened. As the cavalry approached the mud fort forming the bandits' stronghold, the enemy matchlockmen opened fire from the bush jungle and palm grove on the bank of a ravine which afforded them good cover. My father detached a group to engage and drive in these men, while he skirted the jungle with the remainder and occupied a small hill commanding the approaches to the fort. Seeing that this manœuvre threatened to cut off their retreat, the matchlockmen fled into their stronghold, leaving on the ground a few who were shot or cut down before they could enter the gateway to rejoin their comrades. Then, posting a troop to hold the small hill and open fire with camel-guns and muskets, and detaching others to cut off retreat from the fort when it should be evacuated, my father led the remainder on foot and sword in hand to carry the entrance to the fort. The enemy showed no lack of courage. They threw open the gate and bravely stood to oppose the assailants. The dismounted troopers, led by their officers, charged at the gate and a hand-to-hand fight ensued. At this moment a shot fired from the ramparts pierced my father's heart, and he fell dead at the head of his men, in battle as he would have wished to die. The troopers, led by the other officers, enraged at the fall of their commander and in accordance with their tradition that no man ever turned his back upon a foe, charged into the fort and put every man of the defenders to the sword. A dozen troopers, killed in the fight, went with their leader to the halls of Valhalla.

. . . . . .

It is a beneficent measure of Providence that in early youth, as in old age, the sharpness of grief is short-lived, although in the years of our youth Time, the great healer of all, moves with leaden feet. The days passed slowly until I was sent across the sea to England. My father had been buried next day in accordance with the custom of the East, where in all cemeteries a grave is always ready for the reception of the prospective occupant, the next victim on whom death's dark wings would spread their eternal shade. With muffled drums draped with crape, the band of the infantry regiment headed the procession which wound its way through the cantonment marching to the mournful notes of the Dead March in Saul to the last resting place in the cemetery. I followed the coffin, which was borne on a gun-carriage covered with the English flag, a pathetic little figure in charge of the Major, who had taken command of the cavalry regiment. My father's favourite charger followed, the spurred boots set backwards in the stirrups, then the firing party and all the troops in the cantonment. It was a relief when all was over, when the three volleys had been fired over the grave, and the Last Post had rung across the plain, a fitting requiem for the gallant spirit that was now at rest for ever.

And so he sleeps for evermore under the broken column beside my mother, beneath the shade of the cypress and the acacia, within the sound of the trumpets that he had loved so well. He had done his duty!

> The noble steed, the harness bright,
> The gallant lord and stalwart knight
> In rich array.
> Where shall we seek them now? Alas,
> Like the bright dewdrops on the grass,
> They fade away!

CHAPTER I

THE HOUSE BY THE STREAM

WHAT a change it is after life in India to find one's self amid the tame surroundings of the English countryside with its green fields and woods, its temperate climate, picturesque villages and peaceful homesteads, where the people led humdrum and uneventful lives from the cradle to the grave, with little or no knowledge or thought of the great world of adventure across the seas. Those who come from that greater world to live in England miss the wide open sun-washed spaces of the Indian plains where we could ride for miles and miles across country, whether in jungle-land or desert or fields with no dividing hedges; where herds of antelope stood at gaze or indifferent to the presence of man amid crops of cotton and millet or on bush-clad wasteland interspersed in patches with cultivated tracts.

Here in England we have the red and white kine of our home pastures in place of the lean, half-starved cattle with protruding bones, and the great slate-coloured water-buffaloes with long sweeping horns, wallowing in the mud of swamps or staring with hostile gaze at the white man whose scent is repulsive to them. Instead of the white fleecy sheep of English breed, there are in India herds of goats—black, brown, and white—or small brown sheep only to be distinguished from the goats by their tails hanging down while those of the goats stick up.

The Indian villages, built of mud, and often having wide prickly pear cactus hedges growing close up to the thresholds of the huts, are foul and uninviting, sometimes amid the ruins of a mud fort, behind whose walls alone the inhabitants found safety from raiding robbers and Pindaris before the pacification of the country and the establishment of English rule. Round the Indian hamlets kites and dirty white vultures with yellow faces struggle for garbage, as they do in cantonments and bazaars, or wheel in the air overhead, the kites uttering their long-drawn-out shrill whistling cries. In the neighbouring fields great brown bustards with white heads were sometimes to be seen, as our ancestors used to see them in times gone by in the fields of Salisbury Plain and elsewhere in the south of England.

And on the daily morning ride in India we met with hyenas, and wolves and jackals slinking back to den or cover, while little foxes, half the size of the English animal, barked upon the low hills where they hunted for the beetles and lizards which form their chief diet. Then there were the partridges, the grey ones with red legs not unlike the English species, and the painted francolins whose harsh grating cry awoke the morning echoes; and grey and black-breasted quail rose in bevies from cotton fields and pulse, and little brown ones with red legs started from the bush jungle with whirr of wings, while the hares were no larger than English wild rabbits.

There are many things in England more pleasant than the Indian scene to the senses of eye and ear. How vividly green are the English pastures to unaccustomed eyes, used to seeing for a great part of the year a drab and dried-up countryside, and what wide expanses of golden corn in autumn cover the surrounding fields, now, alas, sadly reduced in extent of arable. In the villages in spring and summer we would see the old women sitting outside their cottage doors plaiting straw or making lace with bobbins and cushion, always with a kindly word of greeting in those far-off days. And then we saw the corn cut by the hand of man with reaping-hook or sickle, and by the hand of man gathered into stooks in the fields, afterwards to be gleaned by women wearing print dresses and sun-bonnets, and their fair-haired, bare-footed children. In summer, during the holidays, which in those days were in June and July, we helped the farmers with the hay-making.

It was a delight to suffer no more the great heat of Indian summers when the sinking of the sun is welcomed after the burning temperature of day, when night falls with sudden swiftness and in the hot weather brings with it relief from blazing glare, but often little from heat even in the hours of darkness, and after a short dawn the sun heralds the coming of another scorching day. At the same time the tiger hunter welcomes the approach and the advent of the hot weather, for that is the season most favourable to sport, when water and cover are limited and the animals are more easily marked down than at other times of the year.

Then the birds in England sing as they never do in India, where there are few sweet songsters. The dhyal begins to tune up before daybreak, the bulbul is no nightingale, and the golden oriole in his splendid plumage utters both harsh and flute-like notes. There is in the East no bird whose voice can compare with the song of the thrush or the deep liquid notes of the blackbird in spring when so many warblers enliven the shrubberies in our gardens. But as some compensation for the lack of song is the brilliant plumage of many birds where the emerald green flycatcher takes the place of the sober-hued spotted one that arrives in England in May, and where the bright paroquets fly screeching across the sky, and little flower-peckers flit almost like humming-birds from blossom to blossom.

I had now settled down to English life with the large family established in the House by the Stream, an old Georgian manor a mile from the village, long and low, with what seemed to me innumerable windows, although some of them had been blocked up or "blinded" to save the tax. Its dimensions were moderate, but in those far-off days it appeared to contain numberless rooms. There were only three floors, the top one consisting of a great attic running the whole length of the house with a bedroom partioned off at one end for us elder boys, including Robert and others too numerous to specify by name. We had the rest of the attic for a playroom, where the walls were decorated with rows of mouse tails and mole skins, our trophies of the chase. A creaking pegasus weathercock topped the roof and disturbed our sleep on windy nights. On the front lawn was a quaint old sundial with an inscription which to older and more thoughtful people might open up an extensive vista of philosophical reflection: "Time goes!" you say, "ah, no! Time stays, we go!" But to us it conveyed no meaning. A great walnut tree grew on the lawn, reaching up to the windows of the schoolroom on the first floor where the governess taught her charges and where we all had tea. Beyond the lawn and the garden was a spinney inhabited by innumerable birds and swarming with squirrels so tame that they used to come into the house to be fed and to run up and down the dining-room curtains.

The whole establishment used to file in to morning prayers in the dining-room before breakfast, when we elder ones took it in turn to read the lesson for the day. While kneeling at prayers I would look out of the window through the back of my chair and watch for birds and animals and anything of interest in the garden outside. The squirrels would scamper across the lawn, and one day I saw a half-paralysed rabbit pursued by a stoat, dragging its painful way along the path; immediately prayers were over we rushed out, but too late to save the victim which lay dead with bitten throat. Then on another morning a peregrine falcon sailed on motionless wings across the garden, so low down that I could distinguish all the markings on its breast. Moorhens from the pond walked about the lawn, and thrushes would break the snail shells on the path; it was an event when a green or a spotted woodpecker climbed the trunk of the old apple tree, searching the crevices for insects and when the green woodpecker with its scarlet crest searched the lawn for prey, while jays and many other birds were also seen. On Sunday mornings we all trooped to church, the whole village congregation rising to their feet as we went to the family pew, perhaps as a tribute to the numerous progeny or to the military glory of their father. In those days the country people were happier than those who lived in towns, as indeed they may well be now.

A hundred yards from the house at the foot of the garden the stream ran not only through the adjacent fields and far into the distant meadows and woods, but runs to-day like a silver thread through all the happy memories of boyhood. In its waters and on its banks we used to spend the greater part of the day in summer, running and wading barefooted and catching with our hands the stone-loach, miller's thumbs or bullheads, and crayfish lying under flat stones were seized behind the head between thumb and finger in order to avoid formidable claws. We would work like beavers and build fine dams across the brook, plastering them with clay from the banks. Then we spent many summer days wading up-stream in pursuit of trout, until we became most expert at "tickling" them with our hands, feeling their slim bodies with the slightest and most delicate touch, and then grappling them when the gills and head were reached where they lay beside logs and stones or in holes and hollows under the shelving banks. Gradually, in search of fish, we strayed far afield beyond the garden and meadow in front, following the stream through dense woods where we could exercise our skill without fear of disturbance. Many a time in the summer holidays we sallied forth at dawn, we three elder ones of whom it was the task of the youngest to carry the basket of food, soon to be emptied of its contents and brought back in the evening laden with fine speckled trout; and sometimes we caught both trout and eels on night lines. Then we would build one of our well-constructed dams, with foundations of stones and logs plastered over with smooth blue clay, above a pool we knew to be well-stocked with trout, but too deep for the tickling method; we then diverted the course of the stream so that the pool ran low until we could bail out the remaining water in buckets and capture the stranded fish.

Alas! The stream is not now what it was. In these days of progress most of the trees have been cut down, and the neighbouring town has extended like an octopus, covering the land with tentacles of roads and little dwellings built where there used to be fields and fine elms, beeches, and oaks, while many of the beautiful hedgerows have disappeared. The stream has been dammed to form reservoirs for the insatiable town, and poisoned by surface drains from tarred roads and petrol and oil from filling stations, and garages, and other evils far more destructive than the young poachers of bygone years; the fish that used to dart to and fro are no more, only the sluggish crayfish thrive and remain impervious to these advantages of modern life.

Thus we acquired a thorough knowledge of all beasts, birds, fishes and insects that inhabited the countryside and its waters, and were keen on all forms of sport, a term which in those days scarcely included the playing of games, most of which, except rugby football, were too slow or organised for our ardent natures. In England the child whose early years have been spent in India undergoes a complete change of life. He misses the military surroundings and activity, the horse to ride forth upon at break of day, the wild country to be ranged over in the pursuit or observation of game. But fortunately youth is adaptable and soon becomes reconciled to change; fresh interests quickly arise to obliterate at any rate for the time the memories attached to other ways and pursuits, although habits and impressions may return with renewed or deepening force in after years. Companions of like age and tastes take the place of those with whom the child has been accustomed to associate; the necessities of education come to occupy time and mental effort. In fact, the boy soon adapts himself to new surroundings.

But Robert and I had to go to school as soon as possible so that in due course we might qualify in order to follow in our forebears' footsteps, for in those days it seldom entered the head of a soldier's son to be anything but a soldier. The love and pursuit of money had not infected the families from which the majority of the officers of the Queen's Army and the Royal Navy were drawn. We inherited little or nothing from our forebears except what the historian has termed " the barren heritage of the sword," and we desired nothing more than to earn enough to live upon in a somewhat hard career and the opportunity to pursue a life of adventure to which we had always looked forward. The poorer or larger families sent their sons to the Indian Army, while those with some little income of their own would remain in the English regiments of the line should they desire to do so. But above all we thought that no man had really lived who had not seen war or hunted great and savage beasts.

The time soon came to go away to school, but in the meantime, and afterwards during our holidays, we ran wild about the country in the neighbourhood of our home. Education may have been backward, or neglected according to the common and erroneous idea that it is limited to " book-learning." But practical knowledge gained from observation of nature and the ways of mankind in country rather than in towns, and from living in great spaces where one is free to wander, may be of no less importance. It is common to find people with no knowledge of or interest in the natural objects that surround them, whether of animal or plant life, or of the sermons in stones that are sealed within the iron hills or lie open to the eyes of all who have eyes to see, and who in fossil shell or in the ripple and pitted rain marks on sandstone can see in imagination the primeval seas that once beat upon lonely shores where there are now great mountains and deserts, or green hills, or fertile plains and fields. From an interest in the works of nature the child, who is father of the man he becomes in due course, may acquire the widest outlook on life and the ability to make the best of things in the great world and the greater sphere of imagination in which he lives from the cradle to the grave. Surely the works of nature are more instructive than, if not vastly superior to, the works of man. And so we ran wild in God's own country—the green fields, the sombre woods, the stream, haunted by water voles and small black shrews, that flowed between high banks, over stony shallows, or dropped in falls beneath which the water ouzel built its mossy nest, or slept in silent pools where the quick fishes darted to and fro to hide under the shelter of stones or in holes when our shadows fell on the surface of the brook.

The stream was a perpetual joy. It runs through the whole course of life, often to be called to mind in the remote places of the earth and amid many more exciting scenes of adventure. Then sometimes there would be an excursion to a distant reservoir when, passing through the still sleeping town at four o'clock on a summer's morning, bearing our basket of food for the day, we would walk out five or six miles to make a great capture of perch and other coarse fish with rod and line. We knew the haunts of all birds to be found in the neighbourhood, and could identify them by their appearance, flight, song, notes, and nests. We knew where to seek their nests, but we took few eggs, generally one or two of each kind where collectors nowadays take numbers of whole clutches, but we left the birds in peace to hatch out and bring up their young during spring and summer. We climbed quarries for the nests of jackdaws, rock pigeons, and barn owls. In the thorn trees and firs we found the domed nests of magpies and the platforms of jays, wood pigeons, and turtle doves, while those of carrion crows, now so greatly increased in numbers, kestrels, and sparrow hawks, to-day in process of being exterminated, were more rarely discovered, and a rare find was the beautiful little moss and feather-lined home of the goldcrest, hanging from the end of a branch on a fir tree.

Woodpeckers were not usually molested, but we did once cut into a tree-trunk about a foot and a half below a hole made by a green woodpecker, and came upon seven white eggs lying at the bottom amid chips of wood; but after taking one egg we nailed a piece of bark over the hole we had made and the birds brought up their young. In a nearby tree a pair of tree-creepers built their nest behind a piece of decaying bark that had sprung from the trunk, and nuthatches adopted an old woodpecker's hole and reduced the aperture with a plastering of clay. We knew the haunts of moorhen, water ouzel, water rail and dabchick.

Our interest was not confined to mammals and birds, but extended to butterflies and moths, and we knew where to seek the caterpillars on their food plants. I recall the first sight of humming-bird hawk moths hovering at the honeysuckle and disappearing on our approach, the bee hawk moths amid the bugloss and clover where the bugles blow in summer, the burnet moths buzzing like bees on the wild thyme banks, and the pair of elephant hawk moths locked in love on the bank of the stream. But we read not only in the book of nature, but every volume in a somewhat limited library. With the Old Forest Ranger we hunted in imagination the tiger, the leopard, the bear, and the Indian bison;

and with African hunters and explorers we penetrated the interior of that continent and visited the sources of the Nile and the Zambesi. Military history was a delight, and old magazines such as *All the Year Round* were looked through for " Old Stories Retold," and for the first appearance of many novels of Dickens and Wilkie Collins ; stories of Red Indians and buffaloes by Mayne Reade and Fenimore Cooper were among our favourites.

CHAPTER II

THE SCHOOL NEAR THE SEA

EARLY in August on the way to school, in days when the scholastic year was divided into two halves, not terms, we crossed the sea on a small paddle steamer which was used many years afterwards on war service in Mudros Bay of Lemnos Island during the Dardanelles Expedition of 1915, when it seemed strange indeed to see again a vessel thus connected with the days of my youth. The old paddle boats were very steady, but the seas were often rough and we had many a stormy passage. Looking back now after many years I remember arriving by coach after a ten-mile drive at the school where we soon settled down to work and play and the various opportunities for sport and recreations provided by a neighbourhood with possibilities presented by a country containing many wild features, both along the coast and inland.

The school was an old building of grey stone, battered by many storms and looking somewhat like an ancient castle with its central tower, its gables, and its crenellated walls. It stood facing the sea four-square to all the winds that blow. Between school and shore was the playing-field, and on the seaward side was a spinney of trees whose stunted growth, leaning towards the old grey walls, bore plain witness to the direction of the prevailing wind, and the trees had thus grown so that even on still days they seemed to be bending and bowing to the breeze. On warm sunny days we would lie out on a little hill that dropped sheer some sixty feet or more to the shore below, a few hundred yards from the school; on this eminence, which was no more than a knoll, stood a few old and battered ruins, held together by crumbling mortar and worn by weather and by time, scarred with deep cut names and initials. We would gaze out across the bay, building air castles of which the cloudy battlements were adventures wished-for or to come, and listening to the monotonous and rhythmic murmur of the waves breaking on the beach below—that murmur which has come back to my memory on the shores of many distant lands and through many of those seasons when not the sum of years but activities of action and adventure make up the length of life.

Even so I listened in later years to the warm waters of the Caribbean Sea breaking on Hastings Rocks and the palm-fringed coral shores of old Barbados, and beating with ceaseless murmur below the ruined tower by the Palisadoes of Jamaica, where nearly two hundred years before the wicked buccaneers and their ill-gotten gains were sunk beneath the tide in the great earthquake that destroyed Port Royal.

Then long years afterwards there was hardly a murmur of the waves on the tideless Aegean, scarce heard amid the thunder of the guns and

"the sound of war that dips
Down the blown vallies of the sea."

But many years before that we watched in peaceful and childish days the spring tides wash right up to the hill near the school, which in some ways, though in size, surroundings, and the absence of ruins quite unlike it, reminds me of the far distant height sometimes called Mount Pisgah, overlooking the old cantonment 7000 miles away. By degrees the sea was wearing away the hill whose precipitous descent dropped steeply to the sandy shore, so that some day the picturesque old ruin will crash into the whelming tide, though long years afterwards the lapping waves appeared to have made little impression on the size of the knoll; while the fragments of ancient walls, when sixty years had passed, still stood sharply outlined against the sky, though looking small and insignificant, for as the Chinese proverb says—" the mountains are not as high as they were in the days of our youth."

It was reported, apparently on no ground more solid than that of tradition and of the lively and romantic imagination of generations of schoolboys, that an underground passage led from beneath the ruins to the distant rocky promontory that marked the far point of the bay. The promontory is now lighted, but in those days there was no lighthouse on the rocky coast and we schoolboys saw more than one fine ship dashed to pieces on those pitiless rocks, standing out like gigantic teeth above the sea, while many a bold mariner, his earthly voyages over, found there a last resting place in a watery grave, or his body was washed up on the sands left high and dry at low tide.

We would be wreckers, like those of the Cornish coast, though not as tradition has it luring ships to their doom; but the whole school would wander along the beach when a vessel came ashore, to see what we could pick up. I cannot remember that we found anything worth having; but on one occasion a ship from Spain laden with oranges was cast upon the rocks and the shore was strewn with fruit, but all spoilt by the salt water. Well do I remember looking with lively curiosity through a hole in the door of a barn where the body of a drowned sailor was said to have been laid, no doubt to await an inquest ; but we saw nothing except the tarpaulin that covered the corpse fortunately, for the sea swarmed with lobsters and crabs and the sight would have been grisly and horrifying.

Life at school has left many pleasant, but some disagreeable memories, although these latter have a tendency to fade with the lapse of years, while the good stands out in the memory, perhaps unduly in proportion to all else. The food was so wanting in both quantity and quality that, when the very meagre pocket-money of those days was all spent, we used to eke out our scanty diet with raw turnips gathered in the fields. As long as we had money in our pockets we could buy fine potato cakes for twopence each, a very satisfying food like large thick pancakes ; they were spread with butter and a topping of moist brown sugar, rolled up and held in the fist while they were eaten piping hot. They must have been very good, for to this day I well recall the delightful flavour and satisfying bulk of the potato cake, especially after a bathe in the sea close by before we adjourned to the tuck shop where the proprietor was known as Mother.

Then there were twopenny jam tarts and jam puffs known as pennies ; both named from their price. At another tuck shop nearer the town, fine pickled herrings and bread and butter were to be had for a few pence. We used to bathe in the sea below the school, a hundred and more boys at a time. In those innocent days we went in stark naked, for little boys under fourteen did not cover their bodies with garments when bathing. We trooped down to the sea and undressed on the shingle and crowded into the water without a thought about nudity, although in these modern prudish days, the smallest infants are fully clothed when bathing as though there is something indecent in the sight of their naked little bodies. Is what a poet has described as " Love without his wings " any more improper than when wings or clothes adorn or disfigure him ! Older boys wore bathing slips round their middles.

It has been said that the food provided was scanty. At breakfast and tea we were allowed unlimited dry bread, not infrequently having a bitter flavour, but each boy had only a small portion of butter, perhaps an inch square and a quarter of an inch thick. Tea ready mixed with milk and sugar was served in big tin kettles at each end of the tables. For midday dinner there were great joints of beef, not of the best quality, looking, we thought, like horseflesh, and suet puddings. However, in those days there were few luxuries in our homes ; we throve on this diet and there was little sickness in the school or in the home beyond the usual infantile ailments and epidemics. Only one out of some three hundred and fifty boys wore glasses, which made him so conspicuous that he was called " gig-lamps." Pocket money did not go far ; sixpence a week went in necessary food about six minutes after its receipt on Saturday, a penny packet of toffee known as knobs being kept for consumption in Sunday chapel. But in winter part of the pocket money would be spent on blue cocked-hat papers of moist brown sugar to be spread on bread toasted by the schoolroom fire. Schools were probably, at least, as healthy physically and morally as in the twentieth century, if we may judge from recent books dealing with public school life.

D

My particular friends besides Robert had the same sporting instincts as ourselves. One of them, a fine shot with a catapult, would bring down a sitting sparrow almost every time at twenty yards' range. I met him fifty years afterwards in the war when he was a white-bearded naval officer. The other principal fellow-sportsman, returning like a homing pigeon to the scenes of his youth, died some fifty years later after a strenuous career in America, where he was in the wild West for the greater part of his life; but I never saw him again after school days. Our chief amusements were fishing, bird-nesting, and shooting birds for the pot, all of us being proficient with the catapult for which we used to cut naturally-formed forks from trees and shrubs, sport being varied according to the season of the year. There was fishing with hand lines from the rocks on the far side of the bay, where we could see on calm days strange monstrous fish cruising about in the green pellucid depths. Here we sometimes caught great rock cod and conger eels, which were cooked over spirit stoves and devoured in the dormitory in the dead of night, but leathery conger was almost too tough even for strong teeth and voracious appetites.

Then there was the trout stream where in addition to small trout we found eels and flounders. Fresh water fish were sometimes caught with a worm when the stream was in spate, but more were tickled or transfixed, in the case of eels and flat-fish by three-pronged forks tied on sticks, and I well remember two fine sea-trout, one weighing five or six pounds, being driven into shallow water and done to death with stones. Blackbirds and other feathered inhabitants of the hedgerows were shot with clay marbles or stones propelled from catapults, the " game " being afterwards plucked and cooked over the schoolroom gas. When hunting, two of us would move along one on each side of a hedge, and when a bird was seen to enter the cover we would race to the spot where the victim was thus caught between two fires and, unable to leave the shelter of the hedge, was shot from one side or the other.

At night we would go out with bull's-eye lanterns to search the forks of trees where birds were found roosting and were killed with sticks. It was a cruel sport, fortunately not attended with any great success, but necessity knows no law, and like savages hungry boys had to pick up a living as they could; the "bags" made with sticks or catapults were never very large. The larder was added to by the capture of crabs found under heavy stones and periwinkles cooked and picked out with a pin on the seashore at low tide. In fact, in these pursuits we led the life of primitive man, the hunting animal, from whom we are all descended and from whom hunting instincts are likely to be inherited.

In spring and summer we would spend most of our spare time looking for birds' nests, and I knew nearly every one within some miles of the school. In the gorse were numberless stone-chats and linnets, while tit-larks or meadow pipits were especially numerous, although on the whole there was no great profusion of small bird life. There were hooded crows, known locally as sea-crows, along the coast, while kestrels and innumerable jackdaws built their nests on the cliffs and in rocky caves and recesses by the sea, where Jackdaws' Cave, containing the nests of centuries piled up in layers one over the other, was a favourite haunt. Then in the deep chasms, only to be reached on rare whole holidays for they were far-off, gannets, guillemots, razor-bills, gulls, terns, locally sea-swallows, and puffins called sea-parrots built their nests, and storm petrels and the scarce red-legged Cornish chough were also found.

Sparrow hawks were rare, but one afternoon after answering at roll-call for compulsory cricket I slipped over the wall at the back of the pavilion and ran four or five miles to get to a carrion-crow's nest at the top of a tall tree in a grove. Another boy who knew of the nest also ran, having observed my start. But I was a first-rate long-distance runner and beat him by a good half-mile so that when he arrived on the scene I was already shinning down the tree with the eggs in a tin box in my pocket. But to my delight they were not crow's eggs but those of a sparrow-hawk who had usurped the nest; so the robber was robbed.

The school was a somewhat rough place in those days. Among the boys was a negro from West Africa, said to have been afterwards killed, cooked, and eaten on the shore when he landed on his native golden sand. But according to a later tradition he himself killed and ate one of the junior boys, for which there may have been some excuse owing to the scanty dietary. Another boy who went to South Africa was captured by Zulus, bound to a tree, and used as a target for assegais. There used to be many fights in those days, when boys would batter one another's faces into a jelly, a ring being formed round them and fighting taking place with bare fists, coats off, sleeves rolled up to the shoulder. In these times not only the boys but even the dogs do not fight! We were a virile race in the Victorian Age, when we had good preparation for living dangerously, although life may have been safer when there were neither motor vehicles nor aircraft. In that great era of English history Victorian mothers brought forth large broods of sons to officer and to man the Royal Navy and the King's Army, to win and hold the Indian Empire and extensive colonies, and to open out as pioneers virgin lands in distant parts of the world now too often left unpeopled in less adventurous days. Victorians, and their sons and grandsons who were also Victorians, furnished all the fighting forces of the Great War. For every commission in Her Majesty's Army there were ten candidates.

Victorian women underwent with heroic fortitude and unfailing courage and devotion the horrors and the vicissitudes of the Indian Mutiny, while some saved themselves and their children from death and worse by flight through Indian jungles and others accompanied their husbands in war and on the field of battle. It was, indeed, a sturdy age of a nation possessing self-reliance and independence of character. In hard rough schools and in the poorest homes the qualities and characters of those who consolidated and maintained the English Empire were built up. They governed India and the colonies, established and kept law and order at home and abroad, forming one nation and one people. In fact, virility and the spirit of adventure were the birthright of Englishmen who swarmed back to the cradle of their race in 1914 to fight for King and Country and the land of their ancestral birth as well as that of their adoption overseas.

We who were brought up to serve the Queen and England were ready and eager to go about our work in distant lands. We did not look for wealth or ease at home, but turned our eyes and our thoughts to East or 'West, to other continents or islands in those quarters of the globe which held for us the prospect of adventurous and varied life. Strong men in thousands left their homes and in distant lands cleared forests and occupied wastes where half the convex world intrudes between, and established for themselves and their families new homes and prosperity, laying or strengthening the foundations of Imperial England, spreading the power and liberties of their race, and the justice and freedom that flourish under the British flag throughout the world. Looking back on the careers of my schoolfellows I can recall numbers who went down to the sea in ships, many to perish in distant waters and in far-off lands. Some helped to enlarge the borders of Empire on Indian frontiers, South African veldt, and West African swamps. Many fell in battle in every continent.

It must be acknowledged that we did not acquire much learning at school, but we had a good grounding in elementary subjects and especially in the English language. Among our masters were some of outstanding ability. The French master was particularly efficient as a teacher, feared yet loved by most of us and was in addition a man of remarkable character. There were stories of his real or supposed revolutionary activities in France, which were said to have led to his exile from his native country. I well recollect his telling me that he was present at the funeral ceremonies of Napoleon in 1840, when the remains of the great Emperor were brought from St. Helena and were borne with magnificent obsequies to his last resting-place in the Invalides amid the ashes of his warrior-marshals. He related how he went to see the dead Emperor lying in state and saw one foot of the corpse showing through an aperture where the sole of the boot had separated from the upper; and he described the golden catafalque, drawn by twelve horses caparisoned in cloth of gold, on which the body was borne in the procession with all the panoply of war to the porphyry tomb in that mausoleum of the mighty dead.

While we were happy at school, we were not sorry when the time came to leave, and in due course we were commissioned in the Army in widely separated parts of the world, for Robert's regiment was in India while mine was in the West Indies. But before we parted we made up our minds to join the Force which would lead to our meeting in the old cantonment, and to go together on hunting expeditions as we had so often promised ourselves in earlier days.

CHAPTER III

WEST INDIAN EPISODE

ALTHOUGH I always intended to enter the Indian Army as soon as possible, it was my fate to be sent in the first instance to a West India regiment stationed in Jamaica at the other end of the world, while my cousin, more fortunate, was able to go out to India at once on being commissioned to a regiment in that country. Together with another young officer, I embarked at Southampton in a ship that steamed westwards towards the setting sun one day in April, our thoughts, or at least mine, filled with the romance of history dating from the time when Columbus, at the end of August, 1494, reached a small island or rather rock which rises steeply from the ground out of the sea opposite to a small cape stretching southward from the middle of the island of Hispaniola. Columbus named the cape Beata, no doubt, regarding it as a happy point on his voyage of discovery. The rock rising from the sea was called Alta Velo, for from a distance it had the appearance of a tall ship under sail, even like the many fine sailing ships that we passed with their wings outspread on our voyage across the Atlantic.

But when the Spanish sailors of Columbus climbed to the top of the island, no other ship was to be seen, for they had all the ocean to themselves. On their way down they killed eight " sea-wolves " sleeping on the sands; they also knocked down many pigeons and other birds with sticks and took some with the hand, for in these unfrequented lands the animals had not hitherto suffered from the destructiveness of man. And after the discovery of the West Indies and the continent of America, " sea-wolves " far more voracious than these harmless seals burst into that silent sea and infested the islands for more than three centuries.

But I have flown ahead of my ship on the wings of romance, perhaps with the stormy petrels which spread their plumes over the great Atlantic swell that bore us past the Azores, beyond the hat-shaped island of Sombrero, with all that I had read of the brave days of old, of buccaneers, and gentlemen adventurers, and Spanish galleons laden with golden treasure lost in the depths or hidden on desert isles. The glamour of the early years of the century had not departed. Many fine vessels under canvas still sailed the seven seas, and our own ship spread her sails to catch a fugitive breeze and supplement or save steam. So we came to the almost land-locked harbour of St. Thomas, a Danish island where English was the spoken language of the negro and mulatto inhabitants, and where evidence of English maritime predominance was to be seen in the ships that were at anchor. Then we passed Porto Rico, with waterspouts visible out at sea, and came to Hispaniola, comprising the Black Republics of Haiti and San Domingo.

Our course took us quite close to the coast where rocky cliffs stood up on a stretch of golden sand fringed with feathery palms. The hills, rising from wide plains and green savannahs, were clothed with dense forests of mahogany and *lignum vitæ*. We were, through the sailors of our time, almost in touch with the days of pirates who terrorised these seas in the eighteenth century. Our old captain related that men he had sailed with on his early voyages and people he met on the islands could recall the survival of pirates on those seas and in their ports. We touched at Port-au-Prince for a few hours, and passed through a channel separating the main island from Tortuga where there was still supposed to be treasure buried by buccaneers. It was a sorrowful reflection that the indigenous inhabitants of Hispaniola, like those of so many other lands, should have been exterminated and succeeded by a population so much less desirable than the Caribs, described by Columbus as " handsomer than any he had met with, and of a gentle and peaceable disposition." When at night we steamed along the coast of Haiti, great fires were burning among the mountains, which by day appeared to be covered with forest and our perhaps too lively imagination pictured heathen rites with human sacrifice and cannibalism round the bale-fires that burned so brightly, and from whence we seemed to catch the sound of distant drums—

> Hark ! From the mountain-side there comes
> The throbbing beat of Voodoo drums. . . .

but perhaps it was only the beating of the waves upon that lonely shore.

To the eyes of youth the dawn of day on the dark blue waters of the Caribbean Sea when land lay to the west was a wonderful sight. All day long the ship ploughed its way through the glassy sea, which at night was turned into living light by the phosphorescence where the surface was broken by the passage of the prow. Towards dawn the sky was lit up by a scarcely perceptible illumination. The

PITILESS ROCKS.

Many a bold mariner, his earthly voyages over, found here a watery grave.

MEN OF THE FIRST WEST INDIA REGIMENT.
Soldiers in Zouave uniform, at Up Park Camp, Jamaica.

stars died out one by one. The sun sprang, a golden ball, from below the far horizon, and as the light was caught up in the west, the mountains of Jamaica, at first grey and then dimly blue in the morning mist, rose as at the stroke of an enchanter's wand from the very surface of the sea. As we neared land, the mist melted in the rays of the sun and cleared away, disclosing a low-lying shore beyond which rose the Blue Mountains, mass upon mass, peak upon peak, all clad with dense forest. Passing Fort Augusta where a guard of negroes was posted, and the guardship lay at anchor, our ship entered Kingston harbour, enclosed and sheltered from the storms without by the long strip of land known as the Palisadoes jutting out into the sea. At the extremity of this narrow tongue stood Port Royal, famous in days of old when many a man-o'-war and many a pirate ship set sail in times gone by.

After landing at Kingston we drove in a mule-cart to join our regiment at Up Park Camp. The soldiers were chiefly Jamaican and Barbadian negroes, with a proportion of Africans from Gambia and the Gold Coast and a number of mulattoes. They wore a Zouave uniform consisting of a white waistcoat with sleeves, scarlet sleeveless over-jacket, open in front to show the brass-buttoned waistcoat, and frogged with yellow braid, and loose breeches of indigo blue cloth with yellow stripes. This picturesque outfit was topped by a red fez bound with a white turban, and a tassel, and brown gaiters and white spats were worn over the black boots.

The corps had been raised in 1778 for service in Carolina in the American War of Independence and had been in several actions when brigaded with the 71st Highlanders, and in battles and sieges and in the year of Cornwallis's surrender. They did notable service in Martinique, Guadaloupe, Dominica, and other islands in the long war with France, trophies of their prowess in the shape of two brass side-drums and a drum-major's staff of the French 26th Regiment being preserved in the officers' mess. It is of interest that on the escape of Napoleon from Elba in 1815, the Governor of Guadaloupe, which had reverted to the French in 1814, declared for the Emperor, but that island was reduced again by an expedition from Barbados. The echoes of the French wars were still to be heard many years afterwards, when a French and an English negro were disputing as to the respective merits of their nations; the "Frenchman" finally succumbed when the "Englishman" exclaimed: "At any rate we beat you at Waterloo!"

There was a sadder history than this, connected with the slave days when over four hundred slaves captured in Portuguese ships were drafted as recruits into the regiment, then stationed at Trinidad, instead of being repatriated as they should have been. Among these poor savages was Daaga, chief of a West African tribe, who had been enticed on board the Portuguese vessel together with his escort after he had sold some captives of another tribe as slaves to his own captors. On the voyage the ship was captured by an English sloop, and Daaga and his men were forcibly enlisted. The chief was a monster in human form, six and a half feet in height, fierce of countenance with a gigantic head, his voice that of a lion's roar with the notes of a brazen trumpet.

On the night of June 17th, 1837, the outbreak of mutiny in the huts occupied by these recruits was heralded by the war-song of Daaga's tribe; the negroes, headed by the chief, rushed forth before dawn, uttering their war-cry, seized their muskets in the barracks although they had little knowledge of the use of these weapons, killed the African guard at the regimental stores, and began firing on the officers' quarters. Only a few officers and the band and mess-servants were present, the remainder of the regiment having left for St. Lucia and Dominica, and while some young officers just arrived from England and the sergeant-major escaped from the rear of the barracks, Colonel Bush and the adjutant Bentley called on the mutineers to surrender, but were answered only by ineffective musketry fire.

Bentley ran to the stables, saddled his horse, and rode through the midst of the mutineers ; he reached the St. James's barracks, ten miles off, and brought back a detachment of the 84th Foot, but when they arrived the affair was already over. Meanwhile Sergeant Merry and Corporal Plague, two gallant old African soldiers, kept up an effective fire from the officers' quarters and held off the mutineers, while Colonel Bush went to the police station, obtained muskets, and was joined by a discharged African soldier who was a policeman, Ensign Pogson, and Corporal Craven. Opening fire, they dispersed bodies of mutineers, and soon the rest were put to flight, and Daaga was captured by local militia and old African soldiers. The gigantic African was overpowered by half a dozen men, whereupon he bit his own shoulder and exclaimed : " I will eat the first white man I catch." Forty mutineers were killed or committed suicide ; others were wounded and the rest captured.

A court martial sentenced Daaga and two other ringleaders to death. The sentence was carried out on August 16th. Dressed in white trimmed with black according to the custom of the time for military executions, the prisoners marched abreast to the air of the Dead March. Their graves were dug; they faced west in a hollow square formed by all the troops and were shot by a firing-party of the First West India Regiment. Nor is it possible not to commiserate with the fate of these poor savages, torn from their African homes and placed amid such surroundings. Alas, for man's inhumanity to man!

Port Royal had a fascination chiefly from its history, and I often went to the shore opposite the Palisadoes, generally with a friend who provided a basket full of bottled beer which we shared. Port Royal was garrisoned from my regiment and had also a company of Royal Artillery. It was in those days a fever-stricken spot where the dreaded Yellow Jack was almost endemic. In old pirate days the buccaneers held high revel there and had collected enormous wealth which was buried under the ruins in the great earthquake. The very name of Port Royal recalls sea-fights, and pirates, and Sir Henry Morgan, and Spanish galleons which figure so largely in history. From this port brave Henry Morgan sailed to sack Panama, and hither other fine gentlemen adventurers brought their ships. But the earlier buccaneers, gallant adventurers, were succeeded by a race of villainous cut-throats and desperadoes who harried the seas for a hundred years, during which many sailed from Port Royal to dangle from the gallows at Execution Dock by Wapping Old Stairs. Even in the days of which I write their memory was preserved in the old negro ditty, heard in the streets of Kingston and Port Royal:

> Him cheat him friend ob him last guinea,
> Him cut de t'roat ob piccaninny,
> Him murder friar and priest, O dear!
> Bloody, bloody buccaneer.

The regiment sailed for West Africa at the end of the year, when my friend of Port Royal and bottled beer days, a young captain, who was heavily in debt to the local tradespeople, escaped his creditors by being carried on board ship concealed in a piano case; on the ship he could not be arrested for debt.

West Indians were very good and well-behaved soldiers, but they had occasional feuds with the black police. On one of these occasions they broke out and attacked the police with their favourite and formidable weapons—razors tied on to the end of sticks. This gave rise to an order that no man was to appear shaved, so that they should not have razors. A man brought up charged with a breach of this regulation was sent by the commanding officer to the surgeon for report, but the latter, a facetious Irishman, objected to this duty and wrote that he could give no opinion as to whether the man had shaved or not. "I know," he wrote, "that in former times the professions of surgeon and barber were combined, but this has long been abolished and I am a surgeon only."

It was strange that in so large an island, the physical features of which seemed so favourable to animal life, there was so little game. There were pigs in the depth of the forests, probably descendants of domesticated porkers. There were alligators in the Spanish Town marshes where duck and snipe were to be found in season; but it was a deadly spot. There used to be guineafowl and quail, but these had been exterminated by the mongoose introduced to kill the rats with which the island was infested. But the mongoose got tired of rats and took to eating sugar-cane, thus furnishing a good example of the evil that follows the introduction of exotic species, like that of the rabbit in Australia and the little owl and grey squirrel in England. It was amusing in going round the barrack rooms at Up Park Camp to see a tame mongoose sitting on many of the soldiers' beds. There was little to shoot besides pigeons, which used to fly in great numbers from distant haunts in Turks Island and other places oversea at some seasons. Some golden plover and various species of waders alighted on the island during migration. There was some fishing, but the famous tarpon had not yet been discovered. The harbour was infested by sharks and barracouta, the latter a voracious fish addicted to attacking the extremities of bathers.

One night a remarkable tragedy took place. Three or four sailors from a warship went ashore for a spree. They put off again in the darkness but never reached their ship. In the morning their boat was found floating in the harbour, and in it lay the mangled corpse of one of the sailors. It was conjectured that the boat had capsized and that its occupants had then been attacked by sharks, and all devoured except one mortally wounded man who managed to right the boat and scramble into it, only to die from his wounds.

Jamaica was very unhealthy in those days, when the troops were decimated by yellow fever, which was nearly always fatal. I was attacked by enteric fever and had no other nursing than the attendance of my batman, a negro recruit fresh from the sugar-cane fields. I lay on a barrack bed made of sheet-iron with no springs and a coir mattress infested by bugs whose bites raised large swellings all over my body. When thirsty, I drank out of a tin pannikin, dipped in an earthenware water-pot placed on a pedestal beside the bed. How different from the skilled attendance of the Army Nursing Service of more recent times! But we thought nothing of the hard conditions of life which were all in the day's work. My good negro batman did his best, but his hands were accustomed only to wielding a hoe. His name was McPherson, but he betrayed no sign of Scottish ancestry, being as black as the polish he used for my boots.

In slave days the negroes used to adopt the surnames of their masters, so although they might have children fairer than themselves and, as the saying was—" Ebery John Crow t'ink him piccaninny white," the Macs might all be as black as that scavenging vulture. Thus those who had a white strain in their blood were proud of it. Why not, indeed ? Might they not be well-born like the offspring referred to in the old Port Royal ditty, sung by the " maid " of that romantic spot ?

> " Young horficer come home at night,
> Him gave me ring and kisses ;
> Nine months one piccaninny white,
> Him white almost like missis.
> But missis flog my back wid switch,
> Him say de child for massa,
> But massa say him . . ."

While I was very ill, a brother officer came to see me, and stood at the door of my room gazing with horror at my shocking appearance, as if with the vision of death before his eyes. He then hurriedly left, exclaiming " Good God ! " No doubt he thought I was *in extremis*. But it was on him that the shadow of death had already settled. I had even then begun to mend, and two days later when I was able to take notice, I heard the solemn and plaintive notes of Chopin's *Marche Funèbre*, played by the regimental band, echoing across the camp. From my bed placed near the window so that I might get a breath of air in that torrid climate, I could see the sad procession—the firing party of the dead officer's company, the coffin draped with a Union Jack and borne upon a gun-carriage, the column of mourners following, consisting of all the officers of the regiment, and the men of his company. It was the funeral of the young officer who had visited me and been horrified by my ghastly appearance two days earlier, when he was in full health and strength. He had died in the night of that yellow fever which so rapidly carried off its many victims.

My illness necessitated my being left in Jamaica when the regiment embarked for West Africa, and I well remember watching the departure from Up Park Camp from my window, where I still lay helpless. The band at the head of the regiment played "Far Away," and even now after a long and varied life of many adventures, that sad and well-remembered air comes echoing from the past. How far away that day seems now, seen dimly through the shadowy vista of so many years. And nearly all those who then wound in column through Up Park Camp are far away indeed, and have marched off to that distant land from which they will never more return. Of the officers I am the only survivor.

It was not entirely without regret that I saw from the deck of a steamer the Blue Mountains of Jamaica fading in the distance when the vessel set her course for the island of Barbados. I left a few valued friends, but soon lost sight of them for ever with that forgetfulness which is common to youth. We touched at the port of Jacmel in Haiti, an insignificant town picturesquely situated on a small hill sloping to the sea. On either side were low hills while a lofty range of wooded mountains rose beyond. On the fourth day we reached Barbados, a long low-lying island with stretches of green sugar-cane fields which lent it a somewhat English appearance, belied by the fringe of palm-trees that stood upon the white sandy shore.

The sea in Carlisle Bay was for half its extent of the brightest emerald green I ever saw, while the other half was a brilliant sapphire blue sparkling in the sun. The first person to board the ship was Jane Ann, the famous bumboat woman of those days, who was laundress to all the ships that called at Bridgetown, and who did a roaring trade in guava jelly and other condiments.

Carlisle Bay was of particular interest to me as the scene of the death of a great uncle of mine who was the subject of a family ghost story. It was related that on the evening of his death from yellow fever, when he was a midshipman on board H.M. Brig *Childers*, his mother in England thought she heard his voice calling her. She went to the window and saw his wraith in midshipman's uniform outside. She put out her hand to him, whereupon the vision at once dissolved. She did not mention the apparition to anyone, but the impression made on her was so deep that she at once wrote down the particulars in her diary, which is still extant. A few weeks later she was at breakfast with her eldest son, my grandfather, when a letter was handed to him. He opened it, and having read it placed it in his pocket intending to break the news to his mother afterwards. But she said: " You need not conceal that letter from me; it is a ship's letter, and I know what is in it. It gives the news of Thomas's death." She then told him of her vision. It was indeed a letter from the ship's captain reporting that Thomas had died of yellow fever, contracted while nursing a messmate, on the very day that she had seen his wraith.

A boat manned by a smart crew of the negro

Labour Corps took me from the ship to the engineer pier near St. Ann's Barracks where my regiment was quartered, on the edge of the savannah close to the sea, a mile or so from Bridgetown, I had a small room in barracks. Here I had a relapse of enteric fever, and had, as during my illness in Jamaica, no other nursing than that of a negro recruit of the regiment.

On a sugar estate which I visited, belonging to a relative, were still employed negroes who had been slaves, freed at the emancipation, some of them old and wrinkled men with white wool on their heads. The manager of the estate was some years afterwards stabbed to death, on the bench where he was sitting as a magistrate in court, by a negro with a real or imaginary grievance. Murder of this kind was not common, but early in the last century a Mr. Alcock who owned an estate and was noted for his kindness to his slaves, was found dead in bed with his throat cut, and his particular attendant, whom he had promised to free and who slept in the house, appeared to be distracted with grief. To this he gave expression by loud lamentations and vows of vengeance against the murderer of his dear master, and his grief seemed so genuine that at first no one suspected him. At the inquest, however, his grief was so exaggerated that suspicions were aroused, and it was determined to subject the servants of the establishment to the ordeal by touch, when it was thought the superstitious Africans would betray the guilty man. The slaves were summoned and made to pass one by one through the room where the body of the murdered man lay, each one touching his dead master's hand in passing. The turn of the confidential servant came. He was told to touch the dead hand, and he became blanched and agitated; a juror dragged him towards the corpse, and the man fell to the ground in convulsions, babbling a confession of guilt. He feared that the blood of the victim would flow to the touch, and so he betrayed himself.

There were other tales of old Barbados still rife in the island. There was the story of the coffins of Christchurch. Many years before this time, some half-dozen members of a well-known family were buried in a vault in the parish. The churchyard was over one hundred feet above sea level and the vault was constructed in flinty rock impervious to water. The entrance was secured by a massive stone, which could be moved only by the united efforts of half a dozen men. It would be almost impossible that the vault could be interfered with, unknown, by any human agency. The first interment was made in 1807, another in 1808, and another on July 12th, 1812. On August 9th of the last year, the vault was reopened to receive the coffin containing the remains of the Hon. Thomas Chase, when two leaden coffins, the third having been a wooden one, were found to have been displaced. In September, 1816, the vault was again opened, and all the leaden coffins were found to have been thrown out of their positions; the same thing occurred in the following November, the coffins having been properly replaced on each occasion.

In April, 1820, the vault was reopened by request, in the presence of Lord Combermere, the Governor, and other State officials. The leaden coffins were again found in a disordered condition. After this no further interments were recorded. It was impossible for any human being to have entered the vault, or to have moved the coffins. It has been suggested that the phenomenon was due to the action of water, but there was no sign of any percolation, the nature of the rock precluded such action, and the height above sea level obviated the possibility of the sea having found its way in, nor was there any sign of disturbance apart from the change of the position of the coffins, nor any disturbance in adjacent vaults. The negroes attributed the disturbances to supernatural causes. Colonel Chase, whose body was interred in August, 1812, was a man of violent and intemperate character, who had taken his own life, and the theory was that the other inhabitants of the tomb had attempted to expel his coffin! No negro would approach after dark, for fear of the " duppies " (ghosts) supposed to haunt the place. The coffins were afterwards interred elsewhere and the vault was sealed up.

There was not much sport to be had in Barbados, but I and another young officer used to indulge in an original form of fishing from the end of the Engineers' Pier. We stood there in bathing slips with rifles in our hands and fired into passing shoals of mullet; the concussion of the heavy Martini bullet striking the water would stun a number of fish and we then dived into the sea to retrieve them. We sometimes took a boat and went out fishing in the bay after dinner, staying out all night and returning in time to dress for parade in the morning. On bright days there were many wonders of the deep to be seen from a boat in the bay. In the sea, whose emerald green and sapphire blue were wonderful to behold, deep down in the pellucid depths where the branching coral grows, were to be seen strange-shaped fish, sea porcupines of globular form, covered with short sharp spines like the bristles of a hedgehog, and many of brilliant and variegated hues. Shoals of flying fish, pursued by bonitos, skimmed the surface, flashing in the sunlight, to fall back after the flight like a shower of silver. Occasionally a whale was seen, and I had a shot at one which was spouting half a mile off when I was with my men on the rifle range near the shore. Once an alligator, supposed to have come across the sea from Trinidad, for these reptiles were not found in Barbados, was shot on the shore near St. Anns, the only one in the recorded history of the island. It was afterwards exhibited at two cents a head.

The island itself offered little of interest to the sportsman and naturalist, the fauna comprising only some three species of humming birds, blackbirds, sparrows, and ground-doves, while occasionally a few pelicans were seen on the coast, as well as a stray egret or a noddy; I once shot a large shrike with a red top to its head. In the autumn many migratory birds of various species, curlews, dotterel, sandpipers, and plovers, pass over the West Indian islands. These birds come from the South, from the Spanish Main, and the South-east, and were said to be bound for the North American lakes; they never came back on the return journey and most of those which alighted in the marshes and on the shores of Barbados were shot. There were golden and black-breasted plovers, a variety of waders locally known as pikers, longlegs, and nits. When these birds arrived in their thousands, the island sportsmen used to turn out with their guns and ensconce themselves in wooden huts in the swamps, accompanied by call-boys to whistle the birds down within shot. I used to prefer to wander on the solitary shore; to listen to the ceaseless murmur of the waves lapping on the beach, and the wind rustling among the palms; to look out across the emerald sea and watch for the coming flight; or to pick off the birds as they rose from the sandy waste and circled in the air overhead.

The shore was unfrequented. There I was as lonely

as a sailor marooned on a desert island. He paces the livelong day on the sandy shore, gazing out into the misty distance; does not there flutter out there, on the far-flung blue horizon, the line that separates the waves from the grey clouds or the deep blue sky, does not there flutter the long-wished-for sail, at first like the wing of a seagull, but little by little separating itself from the foam of the billows and gliding swiftly but surely towards the desert shore?

CHAPTER IV

FOREST AND MOUNTAIN

I HAD on my first arrival in India to pass over a year at a station near the foot of a great mountain range covered with extensive forests whose principal inhabitants were wild men and wild beasts. It was a long and dusty drive from the railway, but the journey was enlivened by scenes of the cultivated country in view on both sides of the road, partly broken by bush-clad ravines and waste land. The fields of cotton, wheat, and millet abounded with antelope, and more than one herd, led by black bucks with white bellies and with heads thrown back and spiral horns, bounded across the road in front of us, sometimes stopping to gaze at the passing cart, drawn by a pair of ponies, in which I travelled; while little gazelle, generally in small parties in contrast with the herds of numerous antelope sometimes numbering a hundred individuals, were seen from time to time moving in the cover of the ravines.

On reaching the cantonment, a picturesque little place with its small white bungalows and roads lined with bamboo clumps, I was glad to seek refreshment and shelter from the sun in the cool mess-house, where the atmosphere was far different from that to which I had become accustomed in the West Indies, but was not without its interesting features. Officers in remote Indian cantonments in those days had much leisure, and time hung heavy on their hands unless they had the good fortune to possess resources outside the scope of their profession, or, what was rarer still, an inclination for the study of history and the art of war or for the acquirement of a knowledge of the many vernacular languages of the country. Whist occupied the place now taken by bridge, but although it was still early afternoon a game of poker was in progress in the mess, each one having beside him a large glass of Madeira, while much money seemed to be changing hands. One player had recently won from a friend not only all his available cash, but most of his movable property, including a pony and trap, in which he had driven off, laden with all the spoils that could be loaded on to it.

On the walls of the mess hung the heads of many bison and deer from the distant forest-clad mountains, and there was stretched the skin of a tiger which a few years before had killed an officer of the garrison. The story is worth recalling, being typical of many similar tragedies that have overtaken hunters of Indian great game, and especially of tigers and panthers. The officer was one of those born hunters, not often met with, who have in them the instincts of primitive man living largely by the chase of wild beasts. He had just arrived in camp near the foot of the hills, and the day after his camp was pitched one of his buffaloes was killed in a valley where the tiger's footprints were plain evidence of the beast's long residence in this pleasant spot.

A beat was organised in the usual manner, and the tiger soon showed itself in a patch of grass in the middle of the watercourse where the sportsman was posted. The tiger charged on receiving his shot, and disappeared in dense jungle. Taking up the tracks of blood, for the animal was badly wounded, the hunter followed, his sepoy orderly accompanying

BARBADOS.

The palm-fringed shore of old Barbados.

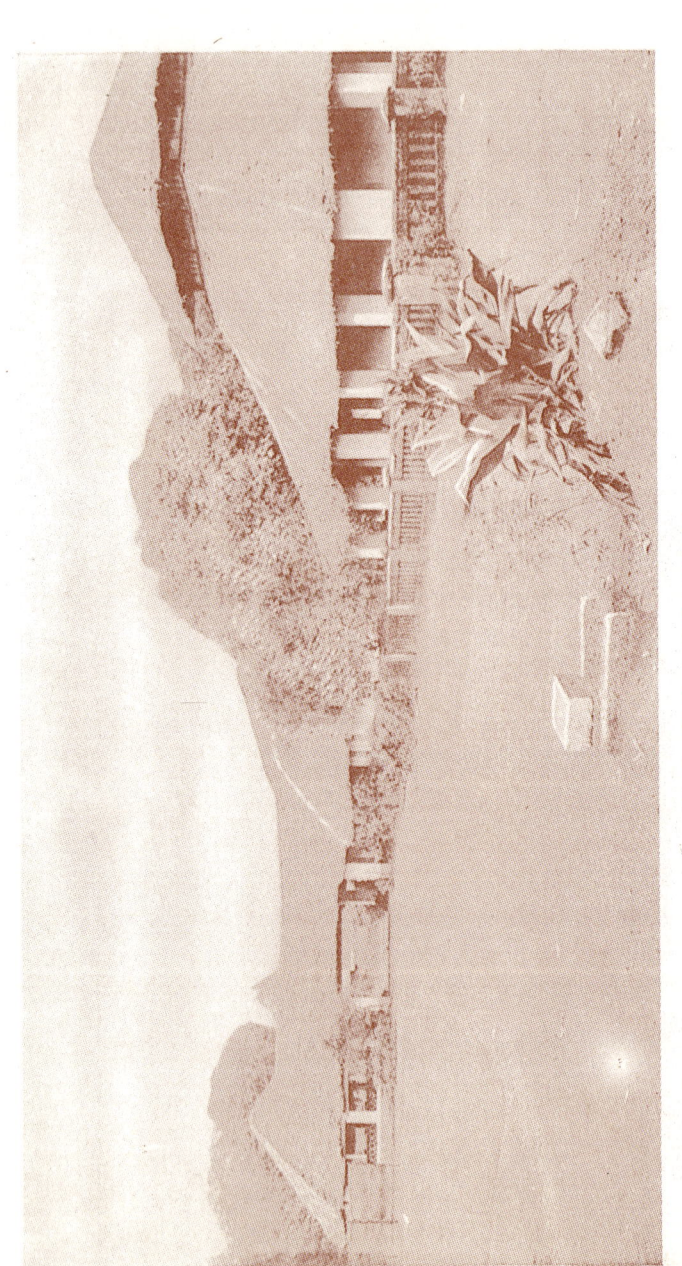

THE OLD MESS-HOUSE.
Officers' Mess, dating from the early XIXth Century.

him. There was a sudden hoarse roar, and the tiger charged from a few yards distance. He first made for the orderly, who was a few paces to the left, but as the officer raised his rifle, the animal's fierce eyes caught the movement, and he turned upon him. Death shone in those gleaming eyes which approached so rapidly that there was barely time to let off two shots before the beast was upon him. He was seized by the upper arm and shoulder and borne to the ground, the rifle being flung from his grasp. He struggled to free himself, but the tiger only shifted his jaws to the thigh, which was terribly lacerated.

The brave sepoy had not hesitated a moment, rushed up with his only weapon, a hog-spear, and drove it through the tiger's heart, killing it even while its teeth closed on his officer's leg. Other men now came up; the wounded man was carried to his camp; he knew that his wounds must be fatal, though they were dressed by the orderly under his directions. He wrote a letter to his father and then lay down to die, passing away in a few hours.

Other tragedies had taken place, one even in the mess itself, where there was the mark of the bullet of an assassin who killed an officer who had passed through the campaign of the mutiny in Central India with his regiment a year before his death. There were still thugs in the neighbourhood, some in confinement but others or bandits still at large, for a native officer, on the way across country to his home with the savings of many years of faithful service, was brutally murdered and robbed. There was also a gang of dacoits under the famous Tantia Bhil, infesting the jungle on the banks of the distant river that formed the northern boundary of the State, and in pursuit of whom our police officer was constantly out with his men.

At last I saw the India of my dreams and in imagination saw what I knew was fact, the distant forest-clad hills peopled with aboriginal tribes and abounding in tigers, bison, and other wild beasts. Had I not said from the time when I could first walk that I would hunt tigers in the years to come! And now at last there was every prospect of the dream being realised. Alas! seen through the vista of many long years, how far off and yet how near those days seem now from the earliest time when dreams that seemed so real were mere phantoms made up of stories I had heard of frays and forays in that wild country. How much of the visions of youth, the long, long thoughts of a boy, were fact, and how much fancy? To me, at any rate, my youth lived in visions is like the dream of the Hunter on the Hill of Heath!

In a corner of my library stands the old rifle; on the bookshelf lie the maps that were my constant companions for so many years. In the early days of my return to India I used to ride out sixteen miles to the edge of the forest where my men would meet me with gun and rifle. Then we would traverse another sixteen miles, this time on the forest road, and always find by the roadside a barking deer or a four-horned antelope, or peafowl and junglefowl, whose sonorous voices even now come ringing down the vale of years. Sometimes on the road I saw the pugs of a fine tiger, which was said to lie in wait and take bullocks out of passing carts. But I never saw him. There were many tigers, but they were not as numerous as I found them a few years later in another part of the country, described in this narrative. Bears there were in plenty, and I shot more than one on the breezy plateau where there were scanty trees, long grass, and black boulders where these black animals were not as conspicuous as they are in some surroundings. Here herds of bison or solitary bulls wandered almost unmolested, while the sambar bore the finest antlers to be found anywhere.

In the course of several visits to this forest, where I would sleep among the lonely hills, I used to roam for a fortnight at a time, but saw only two tigers. One I failed to bag more from bad management than bad luck. It killed one of my calves not far from my tent in broad daylight, and when it gave me a chance of a chest shot I waited too long in hopes of a shot at the flank, and so lost the opportunity forever. The other was a tigress wounded in the evening by the Forest Officer. We took a pad elephant and followed her up next morning. There were plentiful blood tracks and under a tree a patch of blood, and a piece of bone had worked out of her shoulder, showing where she had lain down in the night. She had been hit on the point of the shoulder by a ·577 Express bullet, but it had not penetrated as it should have done, and the wounded beast had gone on into long grass and dense cover. The elephant was sent round with a man and a supply of stones on her back, and the tigress charged out when stones were thrown; with a succession of coughing roars she sprang on to the elephant's head, and having a broken arm, was shaken off while the elephant, trumpeting loudly, crashed off through the forest. But this gallant tigress pursued and sprang on to the retreating elephant's hind quarters, only to be kicked off, when a shot in the flank sent her back to cover. Here we soon found her in an exhausted condition, and finished her off, but by this time the terrified elephant had fled back to the tents and had not stopped on the way.

Bears were at times aggressive and dangerous. One charged out at me at four o'clock one morning when I was riding along a forest path through the shadows and the moonlight, but he went off again with a growl without charging home, before I had time to dismount and get a shot. Another with a cub charged and was killed at close quarters; and three more, a family party, also made an unprovoked attack, the third making off when I killed his companions with a right and left. Probably the dense cover, causing the bears to be alarmed when suddenly surprised at close quarters, was responsible for these aggressive acts. One bear was said to be especially fierce, and had killed several harmless woodcutters. I think this one was killed after being mortally wounded in an encounter with a tiger, for the villagers showed me the skin bearing many marks of tooth and claw; they had heard sounds of the battle and had finished off the bear by casting stones, just as Biblical martyrs were slain. Another bear met with an ignominious end. An old woman, looking over the steep side of a hill, saw Bruin sleeping beneath. She rolled a great rock over the precipice with so sure an aim that life was crushed out of the bear.

There have been several instances of bears being killed by tigers; on a hill-top I once found the remains of two that had thus met their end. The tiger must have been hard up for food, but he is not particular as to diet when put to it. Porcupine quills are often found embedded in their paws, and I once found a number stuck in the back of a tiger. But porcupine flesh is fit even for human food. How seldom one sees them by daylight. I once saw one in this forest at the entrance to his den in the early dawn when stalking bison. Otherwise these nocturnal animals have always evaded my notice. Tigers also eat snakes, fish, and crabs when they can get nothing better.

Panthers were common in the forest; one sat up on his haunches eighty yards off unafraid by the roadside when I was marching with my baggage-carts and was shot through the head, being perhaps aroused by the bleating of a milch goat following the carts. He was a poor starved-looking specimen with the remains of a langur monkey in his stomach. His mate a few days later entered my camp and drank at a trough not far from my bed, but I did not get a shot either at this panther or at a bear which came on the following night; I ran after it barefooted, only to see it pass quickly from bright moonlight to disappear in shadow as black as its coat. There were some bison near this camp. I was following the forest road before dawn one morning and just as it was beginning to get light saw what looked like an immense solitary bull standing by the roadside facing me. I walked up to it and fired into its chest, dropping it with a second shot as it bolted. At the sound of the shot a whole herd broke from the shadow of the trees and thundered off, a young bull falling to a shot under the tail, leaving no mark on the skin. Next morning, on going to look at the carcasses, we found a crowd of vultures and two or three adjutant birds gathered to the feast. Then a troop of langurs gave tongue above a ravine close by, and on running to the spot I met an immense bear coming up hill a few yards off, and killed him with two or three shots.

I killed a wild dog near this same camp, and saw one day a pack of twenty or more of these destructive animals which destroy so much game. This one was shot through the body with a rook rifle and ran off as if unhurt, but I knew he was wounded and would not go far. A hundred yards on the tracks we smelt a strong ammoniac scent, emanating from liquid shed on his tail from a sub-caudal gland. This habit no doubt gave rise to the native story that these animals blind their victims by flicking poison into their eyes with the tail as they gallop alongside. I shot another of these dogs when it came down in the early morning to drink at a pool over which I had been watching all night for a panther. The same night a honey-badger or ratel swam about in the water, plainly visible in the bright moonlight.

A sportsman told me that in this forest he had come upon a large pack of wild dogs which had treed a couple of panthers and were jumping up at them. He shot one of the panthers and it stuck in a fork of the tree, while the dogs below lapped up the blood that dripped from the dead beast. The other panther leapt down and made off, followed by the dogs. In another jungle my shikaris saw a pack in full cry after a panther that had killed one of my buffaloes, so it is quite likely that there may be truth in the stories of these vermin attacking tigers. My own bull-terrier was mortally wounded in pursuing and attacking a tiger.

I encamped on one occasion not far from a secluded pool in this forest, containing the only water in the neighbourhood. To this all the wild life of the surrounding jungle resorted to quench their thirst, and here were to be seen daily sambar, barking-deer, four-horned antelope. Here the nilgai gathered towards midday, the hour when most antelope in India appear to drink. I recognised the same sambar stags day after day, hornless in this month of May. I gathered the impression that all animals drink every day when they can get water, and not only every fourth day as some naturalists have averred of sambar and nilgai. There, too, were to be seen monkeys, and green pigeons in the banyan tree overhead, uttering their soft and melodious whistle. But all sounds ceased and a hush fell upon the face of nature when the panther walked silently to the water's edge. The peafowl and junglefowl scuttled away, small deer disappeared like spectres in the shadows of the forest, and the monkeys alone disturbed the quietude of the scene with objurgations on their enemy. This was not surprising. At one place, where I saw monkeys playing leapfrog like a pack of schoolboys, a panther appeared to have a particular predilection for preying on these animals, chasing them among the branches of the trees. A Banjara told me of another method of the panther for catching his prey; on a moonlight night he would walk beneath the trees where the monkeys were roosting, and where the shadows of the sleepers were reflected on the ground beneath. Selecting the fattest monkey, the panther would spring upon its shadow, whereupon the monkey fell to the ground and was seized and soon devoured.

Not far from this spot I shot the finest specimen of a four-horned antelope that it has been my fortune to meet with, the frontal horns being $2\frac{1}{2}$ inches long. A barking deer from the same locality had antlers of $6\frac{1}{2}$ inches above the pedicle. In the Western Ghauts the frontal horns of the four-horned antelope are usually absent or represented by mere callosities. These animals are generally either single or in pairs, but I saw four together feeding on the fleshy blossoms of the mohwa tree. Near the same place I shot a blue bull in an emaciated condition, its back having been clawed by a tiger. Here also an encounter between a tiger and a solitary bull bison had taken place; the natives showed me the head of the bull, which was said to have been overcome after a long and desperate battle. This was very probably true, for a sportsman met and shot a tiger in the valley with one eye gouged out and other injuries. I found the remains of a cow bison, killed by a tiger a few miles off. The tracks made when the ground was wet and marshy, and the pugs of the tiger galloping in pursuit of the stampeding herd could be plainly seen; the remains of a vulture, too boldly approaching the carcass when the tiger was near, lay close by, killed by a stroke of the mighty paw. In another jungle a Gond told me that he had seen an old solitary bull attacked by a tiger; the tiger got the bull by the throat but was flung off and put to flight.

The range of mountains over which these forests spread their vast solitudes and gloomy recesses, climbing and straggling down into valleys issuing in the fertile plain below, was crowned by massive forts whose crumbling walls had long since been abandoned to the ravages of the jungle and the habitations of wild beasts. They were scenes of stirring events in days gone by. The mountains were traversed by sunless passes worn by torrential rains through still ravines, some guarded by ruined strongholds, and one, Muktagiri, which I visited when in search of a man-eating tiger, watched only by ancient temples, dark with age, where since the legendary days of the Buddha priests clad in saffron-hued robes, sole human inhabitants of these solitudes, had offered their orisons to the deities of jungle, stream, and rock-hewn shrine.

One of these old forts was stormed by the gallant troops of the greatest of English soldiers who, ascending these mountains after battles in the plains below, completed here the final discomfiture of a

FOREST AND MOUNTAIN

brave and formidable enemy. It was said that the garrison, most of whom were killed in a sturdy defence, had cast their treasure into the tanks in the fort; but when these were drained some eighty years after the event nothing of value was found. Such stories of buried treasure cling round many a mountain stronghold; nor has the treasure of Apa Sahib, last Raja of Nagpur, ever been discovered in the caves of the Mahadeo Hills.

In 1859 the rebel Tantia Topi had attempted to break through this wild country with a portion of his forces, intending to raise the standard of the Peshwa in the Deccan and Southern Maratha regions. He was the ablest of the leaders attached to the Nana of Cawnpore, the adopted son of the Peshwa Baji Rao who had surrendered near the fort of Asirgarh in 1818. But a party of cavalry and infantry came up with these rebels in the depths of the forest in 1859, and dispersed them with heavy loss of men and baggage. Since then, except for the presence of such bandits as Tantia Bhil, peace has reigned in the land.

There was good sport to be had in the fertile plains already referred to. Vast herds of antelope, sometimes numbering hundreds of animals in a herd, roamed the fields, and gazelle in lesser herds inhabited the foothills. There, too, was a chance of nobler game. I shot several panthers among the lower hills and one sportsman was so fortunate as to kill a fine tiger that unexpectedly walked out close to him in a beat. Then there were wolves, bustard, hares, and many species of feathered game, while even the rare cheetah or hunting leopard, so prized for the chase by the Princes of India, might be met with; I saw the skins of three shot in the forest and one in the low hills.

In the cold weather we had good duck and snipe

shooting on the numerous tanks scattered about the country, within a ride of twenty or thirty miles, while the migratory quail assembled in their thousands in the cotton and pulse fields. Sandgrouse gathered at favoured drinking places in the morning and evening, partridges, grey and painted, were numerous and there were a few florican, a small species of bustard. These were in former times numerous, but ignorance of their habits and the absence of game laws had led to their extermination during the breeding season, when the jumping cocks betrayed the presence of the birds. Parties of sportsmen used to drag the long grass with bells attached to ropes and so the birds were flushed and shot down out of season.

CHAPTER V

THE OLD CANTONMENT

IT was a complete change from the near neighbourhood of forest and mountain to the comparatively tame surroundings of the old cantonment, viewed from the top of the hill sometimes called Mount Pisgah, which reminded me of a fell in the north of England. From the spot where the driver of the tonga, the two-horsed travelling cart in which I had journeyed from the distant railway, drew up his vehicle, the place presented a familiar appearance. In the distance could be distinguished the group of bungalows, their thatched roofs and white walls half-hidden by the foliage of the surrounding trees, and beyond them the mud-built "lines" of the native troops which I was about to join, and farther again the squalid bazaar showing fitfully through the blown intervals of its veil of smoke.

The winding course of the river, traced by the tall palms and other trees that stood along its banks, could be discerned in the misty distance; far, far away the outline of hills blue and hazy on the eastern horizon; while in the foreground below us stretched the wide expanse of the great lake, now almost dry after the failure of the rains on which it depended for replenishment when half-evaporated by the heat of summer.

The driver whipped up his horses, and we soon

entered the cantonment amid a dense cloud of dust and drove to the officers' mess, a thatched building of primitive design dating from the beginning of the nineteenth century, standing in a bare compound, long since abandoned and empty, the sounds of revelry by night that had not infrequently awakened the echoes now in this twentieth century forever silent. But this was when the cantonment was revisited many years afterwards and found to be empty of our troops. There are to the soldier few sadder sights in India than a deserted cantonment; the lines or barracks are falling into ruins; the bungalows may be inhabited by cattle or by squalid families from the bazaar; the mess where we spent so many pleasant evenings has shared the same fate as those scenes where

> the Lion and the Lizard keep
> The Courts where Jamshid gloried and drank deep.

Gardens have disappeared and taken on the same drab appearance as the surrounding plain. All is still where the trumpet used to ring out across the plain that once shook with the tramp of horse, foot, and artillery.

When I arrived for the first time, the cantonment was occupied, as it continued to be for many years, by a force of all arms, although these were not often wanted for active service beyond occasional employment in the suppression of robber bands. Here Robert met me and took me over to the house we were to share—a long, low bungalow having a wide verandah supported by pillars that surrounded it on three sides. The season was one of scarcity, and there was already famine in the land, terrible enough in its effects but not as bad as such calamities, brought about by the failure of the rains, before the advent of English rule, and after that event until communications had been improved to admit of the distribution of supplies and the organisation of relief works. It is interesting to note that in a letter printed in his despatches, General Arthur Wellesley, afterwards Duke of Wellington, prescribed principles of famine relief which would apply to-day and have been observed on many occasions. He pointed out that the delivery of provisions gratis was liable to abuse in all countries, and particularly in India, and its consequences at Ahmednagar, the area with which he was concerned, would be that crowds of people would be drawn there from other parts of the country, and would increase local distress. His principle was not to give grain or money in charity, except to those who were unable to work, who should be fed at the public expense, while public work should be organised under proper supervision, and hospitals should be established. Those who have had to organise famine relief will recall how these principles have been effectively applied.

Famine affects not only human beings and their domesticated animals, but the wild beasts and birds of the forest and the cultivated tracts, the latter being largely derelict in seasons of drought. The effects on wild life are not as noticeable as was human suffering. The starving inhabitants with hollow fleshless cheeks, protruding bones, and dusky skin tightly stretched or hanging in folds obtruded themselves on our notice. Human remains lying by the wayside, at times whole skeletons picked clean by vultures and jackals, were unmistakable victims of famine and consequent epidemic disease. Cattle, chiefly skin full of bones whose sharp points and edges were bursting through their covering, could be seen dragging about in the vain search for food and water or gasping out their lives in the burning desert and empty fields.

But the misery of wild creatures was hidden from general observation. Wild life is given to concealment, suffering, and dying in secret places, though issuing forth more often in time of trouble, when it becomes tame and forgetful of its dread of man. But the sportsman may mark the growing scarcity of game or its absence from the usual haunts, and will observe the unwonted assembly of wild creatures near human habitations where water may remain in wells although many or most of these have dried up, while little or none is to be found in the watercourses. It may be contained in a hollow tree trunk used as a trough near the village, or in a narrow irrigation channel supplied from wells by the work of patient laborious cattle. Here the wild creatures gather to quench their thirst. At night the prowling panther visits such spots to find a victim among the gazelle trooping down in the hours of darkness, generally just before dawn, or to pick up a stray calf, goat, or dog. His tracks may be looked for on any of the paths that lead to water, together with antelope, porcupines from cave-dwellings in the hills and ravines, wild cats, foxes, hares, and many small animals and game birds. Foxes suffer severely; many were found dead, and some made feeble efforts to escape from pursuing dogs. The little brown, red-legged bush-quail soon disappeared, though in days of drought some resorted to water in the drains that led from the bathroom into the compounds of our bungalows.

But the drought affected the small game, not only owing to scarcity of food and water, but the consequent lack of cover to afford them shelter, exposing them to destruction by man, such as the wandering pardis and other poaching tribes, who slaughtered vast numbers of hares and partridges. The migratory birds, ducks, snipe, and grey quail, were scarce in the

THE OLD CANTONMENT

cold weather, when they arrive in India from more temperate climates; for lakes had quite dried up in many parts of the country. But the little black-breasted rain quail were to be found in quite unprecedented numbers, and hares and partridges were numerous, having probably assembled in the vicinity of food and water from surrounding famished districts, just as human beings flock where relief works have been instituted. Great flocks of sand-grouse visited the few remaining drinking places in both morning and evening. With the great bustard we were singularly unfortunate, but these birds are very wary and difficult to approach within gunshot. We found one frequenting a lonely hill where, sad emblem of the frailty of human life, stood the Tower of Silence raised by the Parsi community who have done so much for India. But this bustard was unapproachable. Another one had taken up its residence on an extensive grassy plain, and one day in October we found a single egg on which the bird had been sitting; the egg was quite fresh, but the bird deserted. The close season for bustard ended on August 31st, and was apparently wrongly timed or else habits had become erratic from the drought or other causes. Then we put up four in long grass and Robert fired at one, but it was lost for the time being; its remains were found a few days later, the feathers proving useful for tying trout flies.

While out after small game we were crossing a shallow watercourse in a wide and somewhat arid plain when I saw fresh tracks of a panther; it seemed probable that the beast was still in cover of a patch of grass and scanty bushes, so we beat through this, but nothing came out. We then found a group of porcupine burrows in the bank of the watercourse, and were discussing further proceedings when the beast came out of one of these dens and made off; we followed, but the panther crouched in cover until we had passed and then doubled back. We gave chase, and just saw the animal's tail disappearing in the burrow. But in a few minutes the beast rushed out, receiving in his back a charge of No. 1 shot, the largest I had, and he scrambled back into the hole again before a second shot could be fired. We could now hear him breathing and growling, but the burrow was very deep and we tried in vain to smoke him out.

The entrance was then stopped with a thorn bush, while we sent to the adjacent village for some digging implements and brought a party of the inhabitants, who dug down from above a depth of quite six feet into the roof of the den. After three hours digging a small hole was driven through, a stick pushed into the den, when withdrawn had blood and hair sticking to it. The men were encouraged to fresh efforts; the hole was enlarged and the body of the panther exposed to view, evidently dead, and was soon dragged out into the light of day. The shot had scattered and entered the body just above the tail, probably injuring the kidneys. The panther was a large male, nearly seven feet long.

In these expeditions as well as in tiger-hunting we found the Banjaras most efficient and useful, although they have been numbered among the criminal tribes of India. There was a large community settled in more than one village in this part of the country. Formerly they were rich, when they wandered over the land with their large herds of cattle, and were the principal agents of transport throughout India in both peace and war. Every man and many of the women were armed with a variety of weapons. Their chief, when asked what was their original home and country, replied, pointing to the tents covering the grain bags: "That is our country and wherever it is pitched is our home; my ancestors never told me of any other." It is related that in former times after a war, when they lost many cattle, they sought some forest inhabited only by tigers, worthless to its Government, and a terror of the neighbourhood, and entered it fearlessly, waging war with its former inhabitants until it became a safe nursery for the increase of their herds. In their wild life, they naturally acquired much jungle lore, and could tell of the habits and the whereabouts of wild beasts; in cultivated areas they knew the best localities for small game. They are a manly and independent race, and we found among them many good shikaris.

One of these had a wonderful eye for country, knowing exactly where to look for an animal. He would point to a hare in a bush twenty yards off. He would bring down a running hare or a partridge on the wing with stick or stone, and he was indefatigable in the pursuit of pig with dog and spear, thus securing the meat that is most esteemed by his tribe. A wild boar is dangerous game hunted in this manner, but a panther is still more dangerous, both from its agility and its teeth and claws. The head of one of these Banjara communities had hunted down more than one panther with a dog of the fine breed kept by these people, and armed only with a spear. Then one day he put up a panther and gave chase; the sun was hot and the beast did not go far, but stood with its back to a bank like a wall. The dog went for it; the panther made a snatch at it, inflicting a slight wound; the Banjara came up, made a thrust with his spear, and missed the mark; in a moment the panther was on him, badly mauling his arm and shoulder; other Banjaras arrived and soon speared the beast to death. For a few days the wounded man seemed to be doing well, and then, as so often in these cases, blood-poisoning set in, and in another twenty-four hours the brave Banjara was dead.

So with the routine of regimental work, and good sport in hunting both large and small game, for we killed some half-dozen panthers in the interval, the months passed quickly until the time came to start on the first expedition in the great jungles to the west to which we had looked forward even from the days of childhood. It was a very hot day late in February, a somewhat strange statement to those who know February only in Europe. But in the Deccan, after the short cold weather lasting for little over three months, the scorching winds had begun to blow across the plains and hills, bringing down the drying leaves to strew the ground as they fall during autumn in England. In the cantonment the sun had already burnt the once green grass to a rusty brown; the trees were nearly bare of leaves except those, such as the mango, the palms, the sacred pipal, and a few others retaining their foliage throughout the year.

Although it was only eight o'clock in the morning, the sun was already high in the heavens, when it is in some respects more trying than at midday, for it shines under and not on the top of the helmet; the torrid heat of day had dispersed the cool breath of night, and the walls of the thatched bungalows gleamed white in the rays of the sun. In the compound now bare of grass and flowers, and containing besides trees only a few crotons and other evergreen

THE OLD CANTONMENT

shrubs, some half-dozen sepoys and camp followers were engaged in pulling down the small Kabul tents, eight feet square and six in height to the ridge pole, pitched for our inspection. These were made of khaki-coloured cloth with an inner lining of dark indigo blue. On active service the tents would be less conspicuous than white ones, and the dark lining was to afford a relief to the eyes from the glare of sunlight, while for use in war they could be pitched with the lining outside to make the tents invisible by night, when tribesmen often attack or snipe the camp. The tents weighed only eighty pounds apiece, so were convenient for transport either on mules, camels, or other pack animals; they had jointed poles, and their size made it possible to pitch them under small trees where there would be no space in the shade for large tents.

At this moment we arrived from the morning parade, and at once saw to the progress of the preparations described. We saw especially to our rifles and guns, the former D.B. 500 Express rifles by Holland and Holland, weighing $9\frac{1}{4}$ lbs., taking a long cartridge with five drams of black powder and cannelured 440 grain bullets, with hollow fronts. The guns were the usual D.B. 12-bore hammer guns of these days. Our clothes were coat and breeches of strong cotton cloth dyed with the red-brown bark of the babul tree or thorny acacia. These were the best and most inconspicuous for jungles of various character as well as for shooting in the open plains, for they assimilate well with the surroundings, while the material resists thorny bush. We had strong boots and canvas gaiters, including some boots and shoes made of soft and pliable deer-skin, comfortable in the dry season but not suitable for wear in wet weather, as the leather is spoilt by water causing it to harden and crack. Collars and ties were superfluous, and shirts were made of light cotton with a woollen mixture. We had receptacles for cartridges sewn on to the front of our jackets, the compartments to take six on either side.

While we were thus engaged a troop of langur monkeys, with silky grey hair and black faces, hands, and feet, entered the compound, where they played games, such as leap-frog, sometimes as human in character as those of schoolboys. Many clung to or sat on the wire fences, and others, young and old, disported themselves in the mango and banyan trees. On the roof of the verandah the little striped grey palm squirrels chirruped merrily, and chased each other out across the paths and up the trees. Suddenly there was a commotion outside near one of the pillars that supported the verandah; half a dozen crows assembled, cawing loudly in conclave in the tree above; squirrels chirruped excitedly, flicking their tails; the little fox-terrier ran out, barking persistently and angrily.

Looking for the cause of the excitement, we saw a large snake with head erect, its black forked tongue darting in and out as it struck at the agile dog. Its expanded hood showed it to be a cobra; of its five feet of length less than two were raised from the ground. Robert knocked it down and broke its back with a thick cane taken from the stand, while I held the dog so that he should not run in and get bitten as sometimes happens on such occasions.

During the day we made our final preparations; maps were consulted, and instructions given to Shaikh Karim, who was to start with the camp equipage that night and march eighty miles during the next five days to the first camping ground on the bank of the distant river. There he would meet the

THE OLD CANTONMENT

band of shikaris who had been sent out for a month prospecting the country and gathering information as to the presence of tigers in various localities. To them he would hand over the small herd of buffalo calves already collected for picketing as bait for the great beasts of prey. Our party was to start on the fourth day, for we would easily accomplish the journey on horseback in two stages, and so reach the camping-ground on the evening of the day when the baggage carts would get there, travelling at the rate of some two miles an hour.

All things slumbered during the great heat of day, when birds sat perched on the trees with gaping beaks as though scarcely able to breathe ; but nature awoke as the heat lessened towards evening. The little barbet sounded its metallic note in the higher branches ; the Seven Sisters followed one another on the wing and on foot from bush to bush, uttering their wrangling chatter which sounded as though they were engaged in perpetual warfare ; the squirrels played in company with the black robins, and with shrill chirrups resumed their games on the rafters, while overhead flocks of green paroquets flew with the swiftness of a flight of arrows on their way to feed on the figs of the banyan trees bordering the parade ground.

Now all were busy in the compound. The bullock-carts were laden with provisions, guns, camp equipage, and all the miscellaneous things required for camp life. Provisions included tins of flour, rice, oatmeal, curry powder, jam, tinned soup, potatoes, and onions, for none of these could be obtained in the part of the country for which we were bound. These were packed in wooden cases, a week's supply in each case, so that unopened boxes were always convenient for travelling. Supplies for the men had also to be taken, for in this season of scarcity we could not depend on obtaining these in the villages, nor was it desirable to encroach on the scanty food available for a famishing people. Medicines were not forgotten, including quinine and the usual remedies for tropical complaints, as well as carbolic acid and surgical bandages for the treatment of wounds, and enough of everything to provide for the sick who might be expected to come to our camp for medical aid.

Two camels, groaning and grunting as they sat on the ground with their legs tucked under them, were laden with the tents, and on the top some of the servants would no doubt take their place on the march when tired of walking. There was the cook and his assistant, two boys or bearers, a water-carrier, as well as a few men whose business it was to see to the pitching of the tents, collect beaters, and take their place in the beats for tigers. They had between them three small ponies to enable them to get about the country quickly when bringing information and obtaining beaters from scattered hamlets. The humblest member of the party was the old herdsman, called Brook Sahib by the camp generally, owing to his European appearance due to his wearing a dilapidated sola pith hat and the remnant of a khaki uniform jacket with no sleeves, flapping shoulder straps, and one brass button. Slung from his skinny shoulders was a string of clattering gourds containing his simple food of parched grain for the journey. At nine o'clock at night the convoy started for the distant jungles.

CHAPTER VI

INTO THE WILDS

WE were up by lamplight and the bungalow was astir long before dawn; by five o'clock we mounted our horses to start on a forty-mile ride to the place we had fixed upon for the first stage of our journey. With us rode the Subadar, a Moslem officer of noble and distinguished bearing, who had greeted us at the door as we came out. "Well, Subadar Sahib, what prospects of sport?" said Robert. "Ah, Sahib!" he replied, "we sit on the carpet of hope; doubtless your honours will kill many tigers."

Robert answered that we depended for that on the Subadar, who had never failed in his undertakings, whether of sport or war. He was devoted to his English officers and to the Government he served. The son and grandson of soldiers, he had that traditional loyalty to the English which is the distinctive characteristic of his class, whose deeds in war are recorded in history. He was a Muhammadan of the Deccan, a descendant of soldiers of fortune who came south to seek adventure more than a hundred years before the opening of this narrative. His grandfather had fought under General Arthur Wellesley, afterwards Duke of Wellington, in the Maratha War of 1803, and again in Sir Thomas Hislop's Army of the Deccan in 1817, when he had distinguished himself in the battle of Mehidpur as well as in many a fray and foray. His father had served well and faithfully during the Mutiny, accompanying the army of Sir Hugh Rose in the campaign in Central India on his great march from Sehore to Saugor and Jhansi, and from Jhansi and Kalpi to the final triumph at Gwalior, where the rebels were dispersed, and his capital was restored to Sindhia, the loyal Maharaja of Gwalior.

Tall, strong, and in the prime of life, the Subadar was a splendid specimen of manhood, his symmetrical figure hardened and developed by manly exercises, and with the nobility of his race expressed in his handsome and mild but strong countenance and olive complexion. The soldiers of the Deccan have always been celebrated for their horsemanship, and he was one of the finest men-at-arms in India. He acted as a kind of general factotum, managing everything and everybody with unfailing tact and good temper, and directing everything in camp so that all went smoothly, whilst in the superintendence of the tiger beat his courage and intelligent direction of the beaters were invaluable.

The road passed through a generally uninteresting country where, except for the numerous antelope, little game was to be seen. We crossed a low range of hills at the tenth mile, where some peafowl scuttled away at our approach, and saw a herd or two of gazelle in the distance. In the early morning grey partridges were dusting themselves in the middle of the road, and a hare pursued by a wolf ran across in front of us, a sign of luck to come. Some jackals were viewed slinking off to cover as the sun rose higher, and beautiful black buck stood gazing at us, while a great bustard flapped off with ceaseless beat of wings to some distant feeding ground. Otherwise the journey of forty miles was not very interest-

INTO THE WILDS

ing, and we were glad when late in the afternoon, having halted in the middle of the day for breakfast, we saw in the distance a considerable town flanked by a dilapidated fort which was the goal of our day's ride.

Soon the sight of our camp, pitched under a great banyan tree just outside the town, gladdened our eyes, and we shortly dismounted and rested in the shadow of the tree after seeing to the wants of our horses, the first necessity on these journeys. The neighbourhood had been a haunt of thugs, those terrible bands of assassins of whom we read in Colonel Meadows Taylor's book, *The Confessions of a Thug*. Wonderful was this giant tree, the parent of what was no less than an extensive grove, for its branches had dropped their thousand tendrils to the ground where they had taken root to form a miniature forest round the parent trunk, and its " column-dropping stems roofed with vaults of glistering green " afforded a vast extent of grateful shade for man and beast. The trees thus formed a habitation for many hundred birds, including the green pigeons whose soft whistling could be heard from where they fed on the fruit, which furnished also food for the great bats, known as flying foxes, themselves clinging like foul fruit to the topmost branches. Here too in the grove was shade and rest for countless travellers who had passed by and were continually passing on weary journeys, often to and from places from 500 miles and more distant. While in the days before the final establishment of the *pax Britannica* great invading and marauding armies found rest and protection from sun and rain.

It sheltered also bands of predatory Pindaris, those hordes of robbers who issued from the fastnesses on the banks of the distant Narbada River to prey upon the surrounding country and carry sword, fire, and rapine through the land. Then there were bands of infamous thugs, the stranglers whose murderous depredations persisted for a thousand years before they were discovered by English officers a century ago. Now the banyan formed an asylum not only for the peaceful traveller and the shepherd and his flock, but not long ago the tiger, the leopard, and the bear sought its cool shades, finding a pleasant lair; serpents and scorpions still lurked among the recesses of its gnarled roots; vultures perched on its topmost branches from whence in the bad old days they descended to fatten on the victims of unrelieved famine and the frequent battlefields of contending hosts.

There was in the village of Assaye, 100 miles off on the field where General Arthur Wellesley (afterwards Duke of Wellington) defeated the Maratha armies in 1803—4000 men against 40,000—and where 1500 English soldiers and their Indian comrades fell in battle in order to establish peace and security in India, a great banyan tree where lived a fakir who nightly lighted a lamp on the tomb of an English officer who was killed on that 23rd September, but whose grave was marked by no tombstone. There you may pick up bullets and cannon balls fired on that day when the ground shook with the thunder of more than a hundred guns, the myriad hoof beats of charging cavalry, and the tramp of infantry cheered on by their commander, who encouraged his Indian troops, riding in front of them and calling on them in their own language to advance.

Every town and village in this part of India had its stone or mud fort, fallen into disuse, a relic of turbulent times when no man was safe before the establishment of English rule. In those days the inhabitants found refuge only within the walls of these strongholds, to which they were in the habit of fleeing on the approach of raiding robber bands. These bandits or Pindaris, sometimes numbering a thousand or more mounted men, were organised on military lines and had their headquarters on the banks of the Narbada River where they shared with savage beasts the fastnesses of forest and mountain. When they were " out " they ranged the country for great distances, even as far as Madras in the south, and the Rajput States in the west, plundering the inhabitants and burning the villages.

Torture was employed to induce the people to reveal the places where they had concealed their property. Red hot irons were applied to the soles of the feet: a bag filled with wood ashes was tied over the mouth and nostrils of the victim, who was then beaten on the back to make him inhale the ingredients; oil was thrown on the clothes, which were then set on fire; and many other tortures were resorted to, such as a walnut shell containing a beetle bound over the navel; the hands of children were cut off as the easiest way of obtaining their bracelets. Women were subjected to outrages worse than torture and death; numbers rushed upon self-destruction to escape this treatment. Females accompanied their male associates on these excursions, and exceeded their companions in cruelty and rapacity. It is not surprising to read that the Governor General, the Marquess of Hastings, wrote that the Rajput States, after the close of the war of 1817, " have been delivered from an oppression more systematic, more brutal than perhaps before trampled on humanity. Security and comfort established where nothing but terror and misery before existed ; nor is this within a narrow sphere. It is a proud phrase to use, but it is a true one, that we have bestowed blessings upon millions."

The town was infested by thugs when that terrible and murderous organisation was discovered and its devotees were extirpated by English officers. These stranglers were generally in collusion with apparently respectable native officials or other agents, usually men of substance in the towns. A scene typical of many enacted throughout the Peninsula took place in this neighbourhood in 1830. A party of Indian merchants with their attendants were travelling to Nagpur with valuable merchandise on ponies and camels. Soon after leaving Umarkhed they were joined by a more numerous party with whom they entered into friendly conversation. They agreed to travel together for mutual protection, the larger party representing themselves as pilgrims returning home from the sacred shrine of Rameshwaram, situated at Cape Comorin, the extreme southern point of India, whither devotees bearing the sacred water of the Ganges travelled from far and wide, and deposited the brass receptacles containing the water in the temple. All were armed, as the roads were unsafe and they had to pass through intricate jungle infested not only by savage beasts but savage men more murderous still who might assail them. At midday they halted for rest beneath a great banyan tree, the "pilgrims" scattered among the merchants so that each of the latter was attended by one or more of his fellow-travellers of the pilgrims' party.

The scene was peaceful. In the great tree the little barbet hammered out his metallic notes, and black-faced langur monkeys sat on the branches, their tails hanging down like the tendrils of the banyan; on all sides resounded the voices of the forest—the bark of the deer, the cry of the peafowl, and the stridulation of cicadas. Suddenly at a given signal from their leader each one of the pilgrims cast a knotted handkerchief about the neck of his selected victim, and in a moment all lay strangled in the throes of death. The grave-diggers, who had gone on ahead, had already prepared a burial place; all were thrown into the trench and covered up; and in half an hour after they had come to rest under the banyan tree, all traces had been removed, and the thugs proceeded on their way, the leaders riding the ponies, others in charge of the camels and other pack animals, and all appearing like a party of travelling merchants.

We went to look at the fort, with its massive stone gateway and wooden iron-clamped doors of immense strength, while at each corner was a round bastion, affording a flank defence to the turreted and loopholed walls or curtains. Now the sole inhabitants were blue rock pigeons and mainas, the latter a kind of pied starling. At the foot of one of the bastions lay a big gun of native casting. The fort had been taken by storm many years before, when occupied by a band of robbers who infested the country, robbing the people and killing many, when the English Government undertook measures for their suppression. The marauders to the number of more than a thousand were attacked by a force of horse, foot, and artillery; many were killed and the remainder took refuge in the fort. After a lengthy siege the stronghold was approached by a zig-zag sap, the tracings of which were still visible; a breach was made in the wall by gunfire and the explosion under the parapet of a great charge of powder, whereupon the infantry rushed in and killed most of the defenders with the bayonet. Those who escaped were caught outside and cut to pieces by the cavalry.

The turreted walls were now crumbling into dust, abandoned to pigeons, mongooses, striped squirrels, and other creatures finding a haven in the fissures between the broken and loosened stones. A rusty gun, in addition to the one that lay on the ground, rested on the tottering battlements, and we came upon yet another rusting amid the rank undergrowth that sprang beneath. The clash of arms was silenced forever. Assailants and defenders had long since dissolved in dust; the husbandmen tilled their fields in peace, all unconscious that the earth over which their patient oxen ploughed had shaken with the tramp of contending hosts.

By sunrise next morning, mounted on our ponies, we were far on our way. Leaving the road by which we had so far travelled, we entered a long narrow valley with jungle-clad hills on either side. Our route lay for some distance along the dry bed of a watercourse, in places thickly overgrown with bush; the narrow path then wound up the pass to cross a range of low hills. I was leading when, after signalling with raised hand, bringing the remainder of the party to a standstill, for we could ride only in single file on such a narrow way, I pointed up the hillside ahead and said I saw a small rufous-coloured deer or antelope moving in the cover. Just then the call of a kakar or barking-deer, so like that of a dog, echoed loudly down the valley, and, remembering the knowledge I had gathered in early days in the old cantonment, I remarked that a tiger or leopard was in all probability on the prowl; the bark was repeated higher up the valley, while the peafowl called in a ravine on the other side of the path; then a peacock gave vent to the trumpet-like note of alarm, rose from the bushes, and flew across the ravine to the hillside. " That is where the beast has passed," said the Subadar, " and there is water or there would not be peafowl; we shall see the animal's tracks, for it must have crossed the path between the time when the kakar barked and the alarm call of the peacock."

Robert now took the lead, having taken his rifle out of the canvas cover in which it was slung, and before long he called out that he had found the tracks crossing the path, where they were plainly visible imprinted in the dust. " A tigress ! " I exclaimed, and the Subadar nodded assent. The sex of the animal was revealed by the shape of the imprints of the fore-paws, more oval in form than those of the rounder male tiger's tracks. We now crossed the ridge and descended to the plain on the other side. Here a few wretched hamlets were scattered over the famine-stricken land. The effects of drought had been and still were being severely felt, for there had been no rain for nine months, and the people and their flocks and crops had suffered in consequence. The wells near the villages were mostly dry, or contained the only supply of water in the neighbourhood, except one small muddy pool; a jackal slunk off and some vultures rose as we approached. " There is something dead there ! " said the Subadar, pointing to the spot with his hunting-crop. We rode up to the pool as some vultures hopped away, too gorged to rise from the ground. " Look ! Look ! It is a man ! " exclaimed Robert. We were horrified to see the skeleton of a human being who had died by the margin of the pool, picked clean by foul beasts and lying grim and ghastly in the light of the morning sun. Towards the water the bony arms were stretched as though in mute appeal. A wretched rag that had been the clothing of this unhappy wayfarer, together with the staff that had dropped from the dying hand, lay beside the remains, while the bones were still incarnadined with blood. In days gone by there were thousands of such tragedies in times of scarcity. But where the poor wanderers perished in vast numbers before the organisation of relief by the English Government, only comparatively few weaklings fall by the wayside. The construction of railways and other improved means of communication, the making of canals and other irrigation works, and organised relief in time of famine, have now almost banished starvation and the accompanying devastating effects of cholera epidemics.

We still had twenty miles to ride, and we hurried on as fast as possible consistent with consideration for our ponies. Passing across the arid plain in a couple of hours, we came to a fertile district in the valley of the river, the course of which could be distinguished from afar off by trees and other vegetation. The character of the scenery changed. We traversed some groves of toddy-palms where earthenware pots had been hung on the trunks of the trees to catch the sap that exuded from incisions in the bark; this juice would be fermented to make an intoxicating liquor. A populous village appeared in the distance. We now reached the river bank and followed its course for some miles; it was a broad stream flowing in a rocky bed with here and there stretches of sand, its waters much shrunk in a season of drought. Near midday we arrived at the ford, where we were met by Shaikh Karim and a couple of our mounted men. Splashing through the river, we rode through a small village on the farther bank, and a hundred yards off saw the tents pitched under a group of trees which afforded grateful protection from the burning rays of the sun. It was now noon; the thermometer registered over 100 degrees in the shade, and we were glad to rest in canvas chairs under the trees after seeing that our ponies were supplied with food and water and rubbed down by the syces.

The tents were pitched on a low eminence, those for the followers some thirty yards off. A shallow trench had been dug round each tent and a channel made from the trench to carry off the water in case of rain, which would otherwise flood the encampment. The horses were picketed close to the followers' tents, and beyond them again the carts, bullocks, and camels, while old Brook Sahib had tethered his herd in a group near the carts, where he had taken up his abode. The cook had built his fireplace of stones and the copper cooking pots were simmering. Fodder for the animals and firewood had been collected by the villagers, and a couple of milch goats purchased to accompany the expedition and supply us with milk, while their kids wandered about the encampment. From the branches of the trees hung various articles—meat in netted safes and in safety from both flies and thieving hyenas and jackals, and pariah dogs, those semi-wild animals which swarm in all Indian towns and villages, leather and canvas bags filled with drinking water, which, after being sterilised by boiling, was thus kept cool by evaporation. The surrounding country was cultivated down to the bank of the river and to within a short distance of the range of hills, pierced by several jungly valleys and ravines, descending to within half a mile of the water's edge.

When we arrived in camp the shikaris were still out on their business of prospecting in the neighbouring valleys where several tigers were reported to have taken up their abode. They came back late in the afternoon, led by Bhima the Bhil, who carried a long hog-spear and was followed by Nathu, whose scarred countenance displayed his delight on seeing us and clearly indicated that there was news of tigers. Then came Chandru, a little brown-bearded man, a police constable by profession; Raoji and Khama, myrmidons of Bhima who lived in his village, brought up the rear, all moving in Indian file. Bhima had a wonderful eye for country and was unequalled in managing a line of beaters. Old Nathu was quite a character, referred to in my first chapter. He had followed the chase for close on forty years. Simple, honest, and fearless, he was afraid of nothing, and would rush up to a wounded tiger or panther and belabour it with both iron-shod stick and vituperative tongue, for he had a strong vocabulary.

"Well, Bhima, what news of tigers?" we asked, after the usual enquiries as to his welfare.

"Sir, there are tracks of a very big and fierce tiger in Chichkora, and a tigress is even now in Shaikh Farid kora, where she killed a blue bull two days ago; also a tigress with two cubs comes sometimes from the direction of that hill," pointing to an eminence crowned by a fort that could be seen five or six miles off in the misty distance. It was suggested to picket out buffalo calves in both localities next day, but Bhima replied that there would be time only to tie up for the tigress, as the usual ceremony at the ziarat of Shaikh Farid would have to take place before anything else was done.

CHAPTER VII

THE SHRINE ON THE HILL

NEXT morning we were up betimes and anxious to set out at once for the distant shrine that gleamed white upon the mountain-top. Peafowl were calling loudly in the cover on the river bank, where these fine birds assembled in large numbers wherever there was shade and water. Overhead green paroquets flew screaming by in flocks, swift as flights of arrows; golden orioles flashed from branch to branch in the trees round the camp, where the green barbets uttered their resonant notes; in the bushes by the river paradise flycatchers, both white and brown with long trailing plumes, fluttered in pursuit of insect prey; emerald green flycatchers darted from time to time from the lower branches and returned to their perches after capturing on the wing the flies they fed upon; and, sinister harbingers of death, in the sky overhead vultures could be discerned like specks in the infinite azure.

Led by Bhima the Bhil, who carried a long spear over his shoulder, we started in Indian file for the jungle, which we entered by the forest path that wound its way up a narrow valley into the range of hills. We were followed by the Subadar, Shaikh Karim, Nathu, Chandru, and Raoji, the latter a local parasite of Bhima. Behind them again was old Brook Sahib, the herdsman, who drove four buffalo calves destined to be picketed out as bait for tigers, and a small boy who dragged a bleating goat tethered to a rope. In rear of all came a miscellaneous concourse of camp-followers and villagers, for both camp and village had been emptied for the occasion.

It must not be supposed that all these people would accompany us throughout the day. Indeed, I was for sending most of them back at once, as they made enough noise to disturb all the wild inhabitants of the jungle in the neighbourhood, although they walked bare-footed. But a ceremony was in view to which the shikaris, the headman of the village, and all the camp followers attached great importance and superstitious significance, so it was undesirable to exclude any of those who might take a part, however humble, in the hunt for tigers, or in giving information as to the presence and movements of wild beasts.

The procession wound along the jungle path through a deep and narrow ravine that opened out into a great valley forming an extensive amphitheatre, buttressed by rocky and jungle-clad hills rising abruptly from the plain. The trees covering hills, here rising to a height of more than 2000 feet, filled the valley and its offshoots, and were mostly dwarf teak, with here and there a smooth-stemmed pipal or sacred fig, or a giant banyan of many stems dropping innumerable tendrils to the ground. A watercourse, largely concealed by the dense thickets and undergrowth of jamun or wild plum, tamarisk, bher (*zizyphus jujuba*) and other trees and bushes ran down the middle of the valley. At this season of the year the watercourse was dry except for an occasional pool, whose margins bore the marks of a tigress's pads imprinted in the soft sand or mud.

We pressed on up to the head of this wooded valley,

where a thin stream of water trickled from a rocky and precipitous height and dropped into a basin among the boulders below. Two villagers were left at this spot with the calves while, taking the remaining people and the goat with us, we climbed the height and came to a halt in a grove of slender trees that grew on the plateau above. Here was the ziarat or shrine of Shaikh Farid, a Muhammadan saint who had been buried far beneath and long ago. A cloth of green, the Prophet's sacred colour, was spread upon the tomb, the four corners secured with heavy stones. We had come to this hallowed spot to witness and take some part in a ceremony without which, so our followers, Hindu and Musalman alike, declared, success would not attend our hunting. For good hunting the Spirit of the Wild, dominated by or attendant on that of Shaikh Farid, must be propitiated, for here Hindu and Moslem met in adoration of the Great Spirit of all, worshipped indeed in different ways and according to differing creeds in general antagonistic, but in essence comprehending the one great Power of the Universe. As the Moslem Subadar, a man of broad sympathies and outlook, said when we discussed these matters, pointing to the distant summit where the shrine gleamed in the sunlight on the cliff—" Sahib, many paths lead to the top of the mountain and to that holy shrine, but there all travellers alike meet at one point."

At the ziarat the goat was slaughtered according to Moslem rites, the flesh was cooked and eaten together with the chupathis, flat cakes of unleavened bread, as well as some rice and vegetables, and all partook of the feast. Afterwards we wandered along the top of the cliff, interested in all we saw. A vast extent of forest stretched below, extending up the valley and covering nearly the whole of the hillsides in every direction, and we wondered what mighty beasts were concealed in the recesses of the woods. The forest looked as though it should abound in game of every kind, but although we examined it carefully, and especially the open though still shady glades, with the help of our binoculars, we could see nothing moving. Indeed wild life has a wonderful faculty for concealment, and in such a forest, even after the leaves have mostly fallen from the trees, it is difficult to see animals except when they move, and then protective colouration does not serve them until they are once more at rest. Not only do they keep under cover behind trees and bushes, but they blend when immobile in a remarkable manner with their surroundings. Seldom indeed does the sportsman come by chance upon any of the great cats, the tiger or leopard, even where they are unusually plentiful. Wild beasts are aware of people moving through the forest long before they are seen themselves, and they either make off under cover when they know that they are seen or crouch and remain immobile, seeing but unseen until danger or alarm is past. But at this time of day when the sun had already risen high in the heavens, most living things had sought the shade of watercourse and bush; here they would find plenty of evergreen cover in the thickets and under shady trees, and in those cool sequestered nooks where all animals and birds lurk during the heat of the day, when even birds gasp for breath, perching motionless in the trees with wide gaping beaks.

We moved a little further along the brink of the precipice, and looking over the edge of the cliff watched the weaver birds and their nests pendant from the bushes. Below them several great black

THE SHRINE ON THE HILL

masses, not at first identified, were suspended from and clustered on the rocks; at length we made out that these were bees, not to be disturbed with impunity, as they might be by the dropping of stones or debris from above. More than one sportsman has been done to death by the stings of these wild bees, while a whole camp with people, horses, and cattle has been stampeded owing to fire having been lighted under trees where they had swarmed. In one instance two officers were attacked at the famous Marble Rocks of the Narbada river near Jabalpur, when they disturbed swarms of bees by firing at pigeons close by; the unfortunate men plunged into the river to escape the stings of the angry insects and were soon drowned.

There is a similar danger from the great wasps or hornets clustering like sunflowers in the bushes. But unlike bees, which will follow their enemies for a considerable distance, attacking persistently, these insects soon give up the chase. That they are dangerous was proved when a shooting party in the Pachmarhi Hills was attacked and one of them so severely stung that he died of blood-poisoning. It is well that those new to the country should be alive to the dangers from bees above and snakes, scorpions, and centipedes below. From the great wild beasts there is generally little or nothing to fear unless they are wounded or otherwise molested or angered, or unless there is a man-eater about. Nor is it the camp fire that protects the traveller from attack by night, but his safety when sleeping in the open is due to the timidity of wild animals and the lack of any inclination to attack man.

We stayed some time in the shade of the trees on the hill-top, and in the afternoon went down to the valley and picketed the buffalo calves at pools where the tracks of the tigress showed that she had slaked her thirst during the night. Each buffalo was tethered to a tree by a stout rope attached to the fore leg; each one drank at the pool, and cooling water was scooped up and thrown over them, while a plentiful supply of grass was cut and placed so that the poor beasts could chew the cud during the long hours until relief came either in death from the jaws of the tiger, or in the morning in case of survival when they were watered and fed. It was a sad necessity to picket out these unfortunate creatures, but it was the only way to get the tigers marked down in these extensive jungles, and it must be remembered that the death of a calf, bringing about the death of a tiger, would save the lives of many more animals which would otherwise fall victims to these savage beasts.

All this took a considerable time and the sun was already getting low down in the west when we reached the mouth of the valley and turned along the low foothills to see what game we could find for the supply of the camp. Most of our following had returned to camp or village, and with us were only the Subadar and Shaikh Karim and a few villagers to carry prospective game. At the foot of the hills three or four gazelle suddenly trotted out of the sparse jungle and stood at gaze about 120 yards off. I fired at the buck, but the bullet passed over its back and kicked up a spurt of dust from the ground beyond. The party made off at score, when a good shot from Robert's rifle caught the buck behind the shoulder and it rolled over dead.

Shaikh Karim at once rushed up to the animal to make it lawful flesh for Moslems by the ceremony of hallal, uttering the words enjoined by the Prophet—" Bismillah, Allah ho Akbar!—In the name of God, the Almighty!"—at the same time cutting its throat; this has to be done while the animal has life in it, no doubt an excellent Muhammadan law, ensuring that all meat shall be fresh, especially necessary in a torrid climate where even venison cannot be kept or hung for any length of time. We reached camp without further adventure when it was already almost dark, and on arrival interested ourselves in the skinning and cutting up of the buck, whose flesh was most welcome for the whole camp. The beautiful lyrate annulated horns of the gazelle were 12 inches long, a very good length for this part of India, although in Rajputana and Bikanir, farther north, they attain a length of over 14 inches. The female has thin horns generally 5 or 6 inches in length. It is a curious circumstance that while the horns of antelope and gazelle in the north of India attain much larger dimensions than they do in the south, the sambar and spotted deer of the south grow finer antlers than the same species in northern India.

The evenings were still so cool that after dinner we were glad to sit round the camp-fire, where the Subadar joined us and was given a chair as befitted his military and social status, while the shikaris and other camp followers generally attended the circle, squatting on the ground, and the conversation turned on wild beasts and their ways, and on stories of jungle life. Bhima told us that a tiger had seized a cow a few hundred yards from the village a week before our arrival, and had been driven off by the herdsman who had whacked the robber over the back with his staff. We remarked on the wonderful courage shown by the man, although such behaviour is not at all unusual with these simple people who live in the wilds. A tiger on a moonlight night attacked a herd of cattle, killing five cows one after the other. The herdsman rushed up to the beast, brandishing his long iron-bound staff, and put it to flight. The man followed, and the tiger plunged into a narrow river and swam across to the far side, the herdsman shouting abuse after it and throwing his stick to hasten the retreat of the marauder.

While we were talking, a harsh grating growl was repeated several times in the jungle lower down the river, following on the shrill bark of spotted deer. This was recognised as the call of a prowling panther, and the conversation naturally turned on these animals. The Subadar told us how he had been mauled by one of these beasts, which are often held to be more dangerous than the tiger. But this is probably because the leopard is smaller and so able to conceal himself with more ease behind a small bush or in a depression of the ground, and so when a wounded one is followed up one is liable to sudden and unexpected attack. Although the wounds inflicted by the panther are often eventually fatal from blood poisoning, those of the tiger are not only poisonous but often the cause of immediate death owing to the beast's great size and power and the terrible injuries caused by its jaws and long canine teeth.

The Subadar would probably have escaped a mauling had he been provided with buckshot cartridges loaded with black powder for his 12-bore gun ; in following a wounded leopard or panther this is the best weapon, as it is difficult to stop with a single rifle bullet an animal charging from a short distance, offering a small mark and coming with such speed that there is no time to take aim. But while on the whole the tiger is the more formidable of the two, the man-eating leopard may be even more destructive than the larger species, its victims sometimes running to a hundred or more. Not far from the place where we were encamped a boy was seized by a panther when sleeping beside his parents with a party of travellers and was carried off and devoured in the jungle within a short distance of the bivouac, the party having no other protection or covering than their blankets. Not a sound was heard, so stealthy were the monster's movements, but the mother of the boy missed him when the blanket which covered them both was suddenly snatched away in the middle of the night. Fortunately an officer encamped within a few miles heard the piteous tale next morning, and at once took up the trail, finding a few remains of the victim, including the gnawed head, in a small ravine. Beaters were assembled from the neighbouring village and the beast was hounded out and shot, the contents of its stomach proving beyond doubt that the culprit had met her fate.

The question of different species of the panther or leopard has often been referred to and discussed. There is only one species, generally called the leopard in northern India and the panther in the south. The animal varies in size, as do other creatures and the tiger in particular, yet there has never been any suggestion of the existence of more than one species of tiger. There are also differences in colouration. The supposed differences generally relate to texture of fur and conformation of skull, but these are mainly due to age, young animals having rougher fur and a more rounded skull with no occipital ridge; this is developed with age. As in the case of the tiger, the male leopard is much larger than the female. Black leopards are freaks of nature, black and fulvous cubs being sometimes found in one litter.

The ounce or snow leopard, found in the cold and

lofty regions of the Himalayas and Central Asia, is a different animal, while the hunting leopard or cheetah (the word meaning a spotted animal) is also a different species, bearing little resemblance to the panther. It is domesticated, the mature animal being captured in Asia or in Africa and trained for hunting antelope, or rather used for the purpose, for it is trained by nature. The cheetah is caught in nooses, but the young are not taken as they cannot be trained to the chase. The Indian princes used to keep large numbers of cheetahs in days gone by, and some few are still kept in India, but the wild animal is rarely found in its former haunts in that country, and is more common in Africa.

Colonel Arthur Wellesley, afterwards Duke of Wellington, when he was in command at Seringapatam kept five cheetahs formerly belonging to Tipu Sultan, who was killed when his capital was taken by storm in 1799. With these Wellesley often went out hunting, making a bag of ten or more antelope in a day. The cheetah is hooded with a leather mask taken out on a bullock-cart, driven up within range of a herd of antelope, some fifty or sixty yards, and then unhooded and slipped. It generally singles out the buck, leaps from the cart and rushes on its prey, pulling it down and seizing it by the throat. Being the swiftest of animals the chase is short, not usually continued for more than forty of fifty yards. The keeper runs up when the buck is down, puts the hood over the cheetah's head and drags it off its prey, when a wooden ladle filled with the victim's blood is thrust under its nose for it to lap, and it is afterwards fed with a leg or other portion of meat.

CHAPTER VIII

THE FIRST TIGER HUNT

WE were up with the sun next morning, and after an early breakfast started up the valley of Shaikh Farid to see if any of the buffaloes had been killed. Cautiously approaching the first place, we saw that the calf had disappeared, and at first thought that it had been taken by the tigress, especially as her fresh tracks were on the path by which we had come. But the fact that there was no visible kill, and no signs of a drag, made us suspicious. Bhima said that the animal must have got loose as the unbroken rope that had secured it could be seen still tied to the tree where it was picketed. This was confirmed by tracks of the calf for some distance along the path leading back to camp, and we rightly concluded that it had gone back and rejoined Brook Sahib's herd; an example of the necessity of ensuring that the animals are securely picketed.

Farther up the valley we found more fresh tracks of the tigress, and on viewing from a distance the spot where the second calf had been picketed, we saw at once that it had been killed and dragged into the thicket beyond the water, the killer having leapt across a wide nullah with the victim in her jaws. There was a pool of blood, a broken rope, and the trail of a heavy body dragged through the grass. There could be no doubt about the tragedy that had been enacted in the night. The other buffaloes were then visited and found to be untouched; we watered them at the pools where they were tied up, and cut fresh grass for them, when they were again fastened to trees or pickets. I could never feel reconciled to leaving these poor creatures to their fate. The sole consolation was that they had no knowledge of impending doom, while death generally came in an instant after the onslaught of the beast of prey. And when this resulted in a tiger being shot, the buffalo served as the means of saving the lives of many prospective victims of the tiger during the remainder of its life.

We hurried back to camp to make arrangements for the beat. Men were at once sent off to collect beaters from the adjacent villages, and as there were enough people within a mile or so of our camp, in an hour the whole party was ready to start for the scene of action. Bhima led the way, carrying his 9-foot spear over his shoulder, for he knew every inch of the jungle for many miles round his village, where we were encamped. Strict silence was enjoined when we entered the valley, for nothing disturbs game so much as the sound of the human voice; the beaters were halted in charge of Nathu and Chandru half a mile short of the position of the kill, indicated by vultures hovering like black specks in the sky and descending by degrees to perch in the surrounding trees. The tigress was evidently on the spot to guard her prey from these scavengers, or they would have gone down to the kill instead of remaining perched in the trees.

We all halted with the beaters, and a dozen villagers known to Bhima as trustworthy for the purpose were selected as stops, together with such of our own men as were not required to stiffen and support the

THE CHEETAH HUNT.
The swiftest of animals hunts antelope.

THE WINDING RIVER

Down by the margin of the river, the woods are shrill with sound.

line. Leaving the beaters at the point of assembly, where they were to remain until Bhima and others returned after stops and guns had been posted, we now went on round one flank of the area of the beat, posting stops on the way, and took up positions in trees at a height of some twelve or fifteen feet from the ground, not for the sake of safety, but in order that we should be concealed from the tigress, which would not look up but was liable to be alarmed if we remained on the ground in this locality, when she would probably break back or slink off without offering a shot. The Subadar with Shaikh Karim and the remainder of the stops went round the other flank and then rejoined the beaters. The tigress was thus enclosed in a limited area with the guns ahead, stops on either flank covering tributary nullahs and other places where she might attempt to break out, and the beaters forming the base of what was a rough triangle, with the guns posted so as to command the line towards which the tigress was to be driven, selected as her most probable line of retreat when she was disturbed. We commanded all most likely ground.

We were now on the tiptoe of excitement and expectation, rifles loaded and cocked, spare cartridges handy in our pockets, and water-bottles hanging on convenient branches within reach. The start of the beat was heralded by a blast of the Subadar's whistle and a distant chorus of shouts. I grasped my rifle firmly, listening for every sound, and watching for any movement. Perhaps the beating of my own heart seemed to me louder than all. I heard a rustling among the dry leaves that carpeted the ground, and quite thought that the tigress was coming; but it was only a peacock running ahead of the beaters; it saw me at once, as these birds always will; nothing escapes the keen sight of their bright eyes; it rose in flight, its long train of gold and green glittering in the sunlight. Then a sambar stag ran out of the cover and stood on a small hillock listening to the beat for a moment before galloping out of sight.

And now the beaters were coming nearer and their cries could be more clearly distinguished. Then the Subadar called out from their midst, a hundred yards off: " There is the tiger! She is coming! She is coming!" She came along rapidly; we could both see her crossing an open space in the jungle ahead of the beaters before she descended again and was lost to view in the main watercourse. Then a stop was heard tapping on a tree; there was an answering rush and a roar as the tigress broke into full view, trotting directly towards my post. Then she slowed down to a walk and came quickly towards me through a patch of grass and low bush, her sinuous striped body shining like molten gold in the light of the sun. I held my breath, trembling with excitement, but steadied myself as the beast approached.

Suddenly she came to a standstill about twenty yards off, apparently looking straight into my eyes, but she could not make me out, for I made no movement; then she looked away and I raised my rifle slowly and fired at her chest, knocking her backwards. In a moment, before I could reload the empty barrel, and I had practised this until I could do it with lightning speed, the tigress had disappeared in the watercourse.

I sounded my whistle twice, the agreed signal to stop the beat, and called out: " I am sure I have hit her, but she has turned back." Just then a panther raced past Robert like a streak of yellow light, and he fired at it with no other effect than to make it

THE FIRST TIGER HUNT

gallop faster if possible; it was lost to sight in a moment.

By this time the beaters had all scrambled up trees, while the Subadar with Bhima, Nathu, and Chandru were making their way round by a circuitous route so as to avoid any chance of meeting the wounded beast. They came round to my tree and I got down, having handed my unloaded rifle to one of the men; I reloaded it as soon as I reached the ground. Robert then descended in the same manner, and we assembled under my tree. The tigress had disappeared in a deep and narrow ravine, entirely hidden by undergrowth except for a few small open spaces. The shelving banks were overgrown with bushes and long grass. We all went to the spot where the tigress was standing when I fired at her. "That is the spot; see, there is blood!" I exclaimed, pointing to the ground. I bent down to examine the track and picked up a large piece of a canine tooth, proving that the beast had been hit in the mouth. Leaving the men above, Robert and I followed a short distance on the tracks, when suddenly Robert called out: "There she is, there is the tigress!" at the same time raising his rifle. But before he had time to fire the animal, who was lying down about fifteen yards off, jumped up and disappeared round a bend of the watercourse.

We now rejoined the men on the high ground overlooking the ravine. To follow in that narrow and intricate way would have been to court certain disaster. The Subadar with a spare rifle and the shikaris went along the opposite and steeper bank, we followed its course on our side. The shikaris threw stones into the bushes at the bottom of the ravine, and they had not gone twenty yards before the tigress charged out with a fierce roar and rushed up the steep hillside straight at Nathu. He stood his ground fearlessly, raising the long iron-tipped staff he carried, and prepared to strike the beast as she came up to him, for his position was such that the Subadar could not fire for fear of hitting Nathu. But we on the opposite bank of the ravine at once opened fire, and under this fusillade the tigress turned back into the cover of the bushes where we could see her well enough to make out that she appeared to be dead.

I was for going down at once to examine her, but Nathu first threw a stone to make sure that she was dead. The stone fell plump on her body, and as she did not move there could be no doubt that there was no life left in her. We went down to the dead beast, and now the beaters began to come up, for we had let them know that they might safely approach. The tigress was carried out into the open and the tape proved that she was at least of average length, 8 feet 3 inches in a straight line from the tip of the nose to the end of the tail; the tail was 3 feet long. The first bullet had struck her in the mouth, knocking out several teeth and lodging in the back of the gullet; three other bullets had hit her well forward. Poles were cut and the body was slung on them and sent back to camp in charge of some of our men, including Chandru, who would see that the whiskers were not pulled out. These are used as a charm, while some say that they are cut into small pieces and given to enemies in food, causing death in the same way that ground glass is administered to poison people in India.

We now crossed over the hills into Chichkora, taking with us three buffalo calves and a young goat brought from camp. One of the calves was tied up in the place of the one that had escaped. But we first examined the kill, of which the tigress had eaten nearly the whole of both hind quarters. After killing the buffalo, she had dragged it to the margin of a nullah and then picked it up bodily and jumped across with the carcass in her jaws. She had killed it by seizing the throat from below, at the same time clasping the forequarters with her claws, as proved by the scratches on either side. The poor beast's neck was broken, probably by its own weight as it was borne to the ground.

Chichkora was not as wide as the Shaikh Farid kora, but was more densely overgrown with jungle and was traversed by a wider watercourse. Here were deep cool recesses overgrown with jamun (wild plum) bushes in whose sequestered shade tigers could find those lairs they love so well, sheltered from the heat of the sun. There was much long grass, green where it grew by the water, but elsewhere dried by the heat of summer, and there was game in abundance. We put up more than one four-horned antelope, and a herd of spotted deer showed their dappled hides for a moment in an open glade. But we did not molest these creatures, although we would have been glad of some venison for our large camp, and also for the peasants who were in need of food during this season of scarcity.

We soon found imprints of the great pads of the big tiger already reported by Bhima. These were imprinted in the soft mud on the margin of a pool where he had slaked his thirst during the past night. The pugs were clear-cut and fresh, as could be seen at once when we had the opportunity of comparing them with other tracks which were two or three days old. Numerous tracks of different dates showed that the big tiger was a permanent inhabitant of Chichkora. The buffalo calves were picketed, and the sun was already sinking towards the line of hills in the west when we turned our steps homewards.

We followed a narrow path down the valley, more trodden by wild animals than by human beings, though no doubt originally made by man. It was interesting to read the history of the night on this dusty pathway through the forest, for, strange though it may seem, animals prefer to walk in these tracks of human origin rather than through the jungle. No doubt the paths are easy to follow; there is no grass and bush to brush their sides or to wet their flanks with the dews of night. From the footprints impressed on the path one can plainly tell of all that have passed. A panther, a bear, two hyenas, some stags and four-horned antelope, and a porcupine, as well as small mongoose and other inferior animals had left their impress in the dust. Then there were footmarks of birds—peafowl, partridges, and little quail. Where tracks overlay others it was easy to see which had passed first along the way.

Suddenly Bhima stopped and said: " Here it is, here is the *deo*." This was the shrine of the jungle god, represented by a large upright stone, painted a brilliant red and sheltered by a little hut of branches and wattle, with a few red and dingy white rags fluttering from a stick at the top. The goat was dragged before the graven image and while facing the *deo* was anointed between its horns with country spirit, *daru* distilled from the fleshy blossoms of the mohwa tree. I had been told that the goat would do obeisance to the *deo*, whereupon the sacrifice would take place, for there was no Buddhist here to stay the hand of the slayer in accordance with the precept of the Master:

> Kill not, for pity's sake, and lest ye slay
> The meanest thing upon its upward way.

THE FIRST TIGER HUNT

Certainly the goat did bow down, perhaps owing to the anointing, and it was immediately slaughtered, the blood being spilt before the shrine and a severed foot hung up within as an offering. But let us not call these simple people idolaters and worshippers of graven images, for symbols and images, and figures of man and beast, are connected with most religions. Here was no praying to any deity in human form; nor did these good and simple people imagine the stone itself to be a god. It was to them merely a symbol representing the Spirit of the Wild whose habitation was in that lonely valley; and to those who were animists, such as the aboriginal Gonds, the Spirit was personified, or materialised, or expressed in the great beasts of Nature, the bison and the tiger who roamed these remote solitudes and represented in their mighty strength and armature the forces of the spiritual world.

When this ceremony was over, we went on our way, the men carrying with them the carcass of the sacrificial goat, for the meat was not left to be wasted on a symbolic deity. Did not Abraham of old in the same way offer burnt sacrifice to Jehovah, and even prepare a human victim in his own son, until the angel came down to stay his hand! And as related elsewhere in this book, human sacrifices were within recent times offered up to the Hindu god in the shape of Shiva and Kali.

As we neared camp we became aware of a great noise, a beating of drums and the sound of wild barbaric music. Approaching, we saw a procession headed by eight men who carried the dead tigress slung on long poles, followed by the village band with tom-tom and drum, with all the inhabitants and the returned beaters tailing after. The tigress was deposited on the outskirts of the camp, and the women of the village came up to the dead beast, some carrying infants astride of their hips and all bringing small copper coins or cowrie shells, the small change of the country, and some with red powder to place the caste-mark on the forehead of the tigress. They salaamed to the dead beast, and deposited their offerings on the body, where it was afterwards collected by Bhima. Meanwhile Nathu had arrived and, standing by the tigress, described to the admiring crowd with voluble tongue and realistic gesture how he had driven the animal down hill " as if it were a goat " when it charged him ; and how the first tiger had fallen to the rifle of the Baba Sahib whom he had taught to shoot when he was a baby.

In course of time all these people disappeared and Chandru and the syces set to work to remove the skin. We were interested spectators of this operation, and lent a hand from time to time. A slit was made down the middle of the animal from chin to tip of tail and a cut down the inside of each leg to the pads. The skin was then gradually stripped off, special care being needed at the lips, nose, paws, and ears. It was then pegged out with bamboo slips with the hairy side underneath on the ground over dry cut grass in a shady place so that the sun should not melt the fat and cause hardening of the pelt. Care was taken not to stretch the skin unduly. When all the adhering flesh had been taken off, the skin was well scraped with flat stones and knives, a mixture of burnt alum and saltpetre was well rubbed in and arsenical soap applied round the lips, nose, ears, and pads, where there was most fear of the skin going bad and the hair slipping in consequence. I had skinned animals in early days in India, and we collected the skins of small creatures shot at home with catapults, so we were interested in seeing this great beast treated in the same manner.

Meanwhile the " lucky bones " were cut out of the chest by Nathu. These are clavicles or rudimentary collar-bones found in all the cat-tribe, about four inches long and hatchet-shaped in the tiger. They are much prized, and, as well as the claws, often mounted in gold and hung round the necks of children to keep off evil. Great care was taken to collect all the fat from the tigress ; this was boiled down in a pot over the fire and stored in bottles. The villagers also carried off not only bits of flesh and the liver, but the whole legs and quarters. On being questioned, the Subadar said that the fat was most valuable as a remedy for rheumatism and to make men strong when rubbed into the patient. This is a universal belief throughout the whole of India, where the fat of tigers is everywhere highly prized. He added that the villagers would eat the flesh and especially the liver, the latter being supposed to impart to those who partook of it some of the courage of the tiger. " But," said Nathu with oriental flattery, which is really only politeness, " it is not necessary for the sahibs to eat tigers' liver, as they already possess the courage of the tiger." Even so the Persian courtier said : " If the King says at midday ' It is midnight,' reply : ' True indeed, behold the moon and stars ! ' "

Talking over the events of the day, we expressed wonder at the beauty and symmetry and size of the tiger, so much greater than we had thought of. Bhima told us that when we killed the big tiger in Chichkora we would see that he would be twice the size, or at least twice the weight of the tigress, and I remarked that we would realise how much finer these animals are in their native wilds than in captivity, where alone I had previously seen them. All in camp were tired after the long day's work and excitement. Even Nathu's garrulous tongue stopped wagging before ten o'clock, and half an hour later the whole camp was asleep.

CHAPTER IX

VOICES IN THE FOREST

THE voices to be heard in the forests of India are many and varied, whether they resound by night or make music sweet to the lover of nature at dawn or in the heat of the noonday sun. They vary with the time of day and with the seasons. Save where the birds congregate in shady foliage there is not generally much sound, except of insect life during the heat of the day. Nature slumbers soon after sunrise until the sun reaches the tops of the tall trees in the west. In the rainy season from June to September, when the woods are green and the long dank grass is breast-high, the birds are mostly breeding and their songs and notes are attuned accordingly. Then when autumn approaches and the trees assume variegated tints whilst the grass grows daily more sere and yellow beneath the scorching rays of the sun, no longer tempered by clouds, the courting of some of the larger animals, and especially of those deer whose antlers are now mature, takes place; the stags bellow and meet in combat when the clashing of their antlers awakes the woodland echoes.

And when the cold weather arrives, and as it advances, the leaves fall to the ground and the grass and undergrowth gradually die away or are burnt by forest fires, the great cats, striped and spotted, hold their courtship, and the sloth bear of the plains and lower hills are also pairing. When the hot weather draws on in February and March we find many of these animals with young a few weeks old, the bear carrying her progeny, generally two in number, pick-a-back where they peep with beady eyes from the long hair between her shoulders. The tigress hides her offspring in a cave or thicket in the depth of the forest until they are old enough to share with her the nightly hunt and feast. Tigers sometimes live in pairs.

The hot weather is the time for the sportsman. Then the foliage has been thinned out by the long drought, broken only by December rains for a few days, and the forms of wild beasts moving in the jungle can be distinguished where they would have been quite invisible in the dense undergrowth early in the year. Moreover the water at this season is scarce and scanty so that the beasts of the field, impatient as they are of thirst, congregate in or resort frequently to the neighbourhood of the life-sustaining pools where one can easily find their tracks at the drinking places they have visited during the night or in the early morning.

The voices of the great felidæ are generally heard at night, but the tiger, unlike the lion, is not a noisy animal; he roars seldom during the hot season, except when he is angry or frightened or a bullet strikes him. Now and then his deep voice breaks the silence of the night, or if one is encamped in a favourable spot, the loud sigh of the giant cat may be heard perchance as he wanders in search of prey. The panther is not so quiet. Often his harsh grating cry is borne upon the evening air close to the camp or village round which he prowls in hopes of picking up a stray goat, or calf, or dog; and if the remains of offal of game killed during the day should be left

VOICES IN THE FOREST

in the vicinity, hyenas may be heard wrangling over their unsavoury meal in the hours of darkness. All these animals have their haunts not very far removed from human habitations, for there ruminants can ravage the crops, and carnivora follow their prey and also find cattle easy to kill. But the elephant and bison love to roam in more secluded regions where they are seldom disturbed by the intrusion of man.

There is a small bird, the dhyal, which always appears to haunt the vicinity of camps in great jungles. About an hour before dawn it begins to tune its pipe in the darkness. At first it sounds one oft-repeated note, and as the minutes pass, the notes increase in number and volume until finally when the coming dawn tinges the sky with pink and the mists of night break and disperse before the rising sun, it bursts forth into a melody rivalling that of the nightingale. It is the prelude to nature's orchestra. With the day comes the brain-fever bird, shrieking from the tops of the trees.

Down by the margin of the river the spotted stags challenge one another and ever and anon the hinds bark loudly. The woods are shrill with sound. The hunter of great game soon learns to distinguish the voices that denote alarm. Of such is the peculiar chattering of monkeys who will follow along the tree-tops the course of a passing tiger or panther, swinging from branch to branch and giving expression to strange oaths in their simian tongue, and strange grimaces on their expressive countenances. As the tiger goes on his way either by night or by day, noiselessly stalking with velvet footfall in the shady places of the forest, the chorus of alarm is taken up by the peafowl with a variety of notes, from the piercing " Miaou ! Miaou ! " to the trumpet-like call which is always a signal of danger. The cry is continued by the kakar, the small red deer which barks persistently from the hillside as long as the feline foe is in sight, whilst the shrill voice of the spotted deer and the deep-toned bell of the sambar add to the concatenation of sound. All cry out upon the midnight murderer! It is noteworthy too that the monkeys in the tree-tops will hurl abuse at Bhalu the bear.

There are many other voices to be heard in the forest. There is the " Phial " of the jackal attendant upon a beast of prey, distinct from the gathered yell uttered by a troop of these scavengers. There is the hiss like that of a snake from the gazelle and the cry of the fox at dawn and at the setting of the sun. The jungle-cocks crow defiance at one another and the painted francolin utters its harsh and monotonous call—" Shaikh Farid! Shaikh Farid! " from the cover of grass patch or bushes, while the grey partridge joins in with shriller note. And above all, with almost ceaseless screech, the stridulation of the cicadas fills the forest with sound, to be interrupted by silences deep and empty when they stop for a few moments.

But there is a charm beyond the desirability of the game, and in course of time the taking of life in any form becomes distasteful to the sportsman and naturalist; only in youth the primitive instincts of the hunting man assert themselves. The jungle teems with animal life. It is possible that a tiger may be met with, bent upon an errand similar to that of the hunter, his presence perhaps betrayed by a voice of fear in the forest. Bison and blue bull, silent denizens of the wilds, may be seen; the rough backs of crocodiles show above the surface, or perhaps only their evil snouts betray their presence; otters

VOICES IN THE FOREST

chase the fish, giving utterance to strange twitterings. And if you climb the neighbouring hill that casts its long shadow down to the water's edge, you may find a sambar stag, game more worthy of the rifle than the spotted one, or may meet a shaggy and crusty-tempered bear. And then—to rest upon the hill-top and look down upon the view below, a scene beautiful to behold. For miles the river can be seen winding with serpentine course through jungleland and field, and on all sides resound the voices of the forest where graceful forms are moving in the glades and on the river bank. The cry of the peafowl, the bark of the deer, the strident screech of the cicadas, these are sounds that will haunt the memory by day and night long after we have left forever the enchanted forests of our youth and passed away entirely from the scenes of our delight.

We awoke to such sounds and scenes on the morning after killing the tigress. The camp was already astir, although it was still dark except for the phantom of false morning in the east. The cook was at work among his pots and pans beside a brightly flickering fire. The men were preparing for the activities of the coming day; Chandru was giving a few finishing touches to the skin of the tigress; the Subadar was holding a conference with Bhima and Nathu; and the syces were bringing the horses back from the river where they had taken them to water. Even old Brook Sahib was busy cleaning and scraping the tigress's skull.

Robert, with Bhima and Nathu, was to go up Chichkora, taking his pony and a mounted man so that news of a kill might be sent quickly back to camp. Chandru and Raoji, also taking a mounted man, were to visit the buffaloes picketed in the valley of the tigress. But these two parties were not to start before eight o'clock, so that there should be no fear of disturbing the tiger before he had settled down for the day. The farthest buffalo was not more than four miles from camp. I was to cross the river into the heavy jungle on the far side, not only to get some venison needed for the supply of the camp, but in the hope of finding tracks of other tigers. Accompanied by the Subadar and two local men, I set off at once, and having crossed the river by a shallow ford we entered a wide nullah, at this season dry except for a few pools.

We followed the watercourse for some distance to see what tracks were at the waterholes, but finding only those of deer and nilgai we mounted the bank to get a better view of the surrounding country. Suddenly a small animal ran out of a patch of long grass, its white scut thrown up like that of a rabbit as it bounded off. At a distance of some fifty yards it stood at gaze, and I killed it with a shot behind the shoulder. We found that it was a fine specimen of a four-horned antelope, an animal somewhat smaller than a gazelle, and the only creature in the world having four normal horns, the posterior ones being five inches and the anterior over two inches long. These, the smallest antelope found in India, are common in the southern part of the peninsula. Well developed anterior horns are rare, being frequently represented by mere knobs or black callosities, while they are often altogether absent, especially in the Western Ghats.

We placed the dead antelope in a convenient spot for recovery on the return journey, covering it over with leaves and branches to protect it from the vultures, which would never find it when thus concealed for they hunt entirely by sight and not by scent. The tiger and the leopard are well aware of this, and if they do not remain near the kill in order to protect it themselves, they cover it up with leaves or conceal it among bushes or in a thicket. The truth of this was proved before we had gone much farther, when the smell of putrefaction drew our attention to the carcass of another of these small antelope, deposited in the fork of a tree some ten feet from the ground, and untouched by vultures, nor were any to be seen in the neighbourhood. The tree was evergreen, or at least its green leaves sheltered the carcass from the view of vultures overhead. One of the men dislodged the carcass with a stick and it fell to the ground, when we saw from the holes in the throat that it had been killed by a panther. The chest was partly eaten and the stomach had been removed ; most of the great cats tear out and place the offal on one side in a neat parcel, often burying it or covering it up. The tiger begins to eat at the haunches, while the panther generally begins to devour its prey at the stomach or chest.

On the hillsides we saw that the bark of many trees had been rubbed off by deer polishing their antlers, or getting rid of the velvet adhering to them when newly mature. There was here a vast quantity of game. Peafowl scuttled away into the dense cover near the pools ; four-horned antelope dashed across the glades ; and grey langur monkeys with black faces leapt about the branches overhead. Spotted deer abounded, generally in small herds of a dozen or so, with a fine stag as leader ; sometimes they stood at gaze within view ; often they were only heard as they went off with shrill barks of alarm. Then a solitary stag with wide, spreading antlers stood in an open glade gazing at us, its dappled hide so blending with the background that I did not see it until a slight movement betrayed it, when a shot behind the shoulder killed it. The tape-measure showed the horns to be 35 inches in length ; it was an eight-pointer, the antlers remarkably massive and having a long extra tine on each antler near the brow, a not uncommon abnormality. The sambar and spotted deer are of the rusine type, having normally only three points to each antler.

Having covered up the carcass we went on and descended into the dry watercourse to a pool under a great tree. Here were fresh tracks of a tiger, and we tied up a buffalo calf, watered it, and placed a heap of freshly-cut grass in front of it. We picketed another calf higher up the watercourse near a pool among some rocks, where grass and bushes would provide cover for the tiger if a kill took place. This system of picketing out an unfortunate animal as bait for tigers may seem cruel. But it is necessary, for in these great forests and extensive jungles it would otherwise be impossible to mark down the game and so bring it to bag, the natural habit of the tiger being to lie up near his prey. The patient beasts do not appear to suffer ; in most cases death comes very quickly from the furious attack of a ravening beast ; one has been known to get up and resume chewing the cud immediately after being knocked down and wounded by a tiger. Moreover, one buffalo dies to save many other animals destined to be killed and devoured if tigers were not hunted and slain. Many thousands of cattle are killed annually by tigers and panthers ; and in the case of a man-eater the death of a calf may save many human lives.

The sun had by now climbed high in the heavens and we turned homewards in expectation of finding Robert back in camp with news of what had happened during the night in Chichkora. We reached camp simultaneously with the other parties. Chandru reported that there had been a kill by a tiger in the Shaihk Farid Kora, and Robert related his adventures in Chichkora. When he and Bhima arrived within sight of the spot where the first buffalo was picketed, they were greeted with grunts of welcome from the patient beast. Nearing the second bait, they saw a crow on the branch of a tree on the bank above, cawing vociferously and evidently alarmed or irritated by something in the nullah below. Bhima said that without doubt there had been a kill, and that the tiger was on the spot.

Cautiously climbing a tree fixed upon already as the one to view the kill from, Bhima announced that the buffalo had been killed and that he could see from the tracks of the drag that the tiger had taken it up into some dense cover in a small tributary that came down to join the main channel from the hills above. The mounted man was at once sent back to camp with the news and instructions to see to the assembling of beaters, while Robert and Bhima went on towards the head of the valley to look at the remaining picketed calf. This also had been killed and dragged into a dense and extensive thicket of bushes and elephant grass.

In these covers it was not possible to move about, or the hunter might try to stalk the beast and get a shot in that way. But to prowl about in such dense jungle on the faint chance of getting a glimpse of the game would be useless; the tiger would be disturbed by the noise inseparable from such procedure, and would slip away without exposing itself to view. The only feasible method of bringing the game to bag would be to drive it out of the thicket with beaters.

The party now turned back towards camp, Robert on his pony while Bhima led the way and the syce carried the rifle. They traversed the path by which they had come, when suddenly Bhima stopped and pointed to a track in the dusty surface. Robert jumped off his pony and saw the pugs of the big tiger freshly imprinted on the path. The spot where they stood was some three hundred yards above the first kill.

"Look, Sahib!" exclaimed Bhima: "the tiger has been following us!" And indeed he had walked after them up the path, for the tracks were not there when they came and now overlay their footmarks. Pointing with his spear farther on, Bhima added: "See, he has turned into the jungle, and no doubt gone back to his kill."

The path was roughly parallel to the watercourse and about sixty yards from it. It appeared that the tiger, himself unseen, must have observed them near his prey and had followed them for some three hundred yards, not with any evil intent, for he was no man-eater, but merely to see them off his premises. He might have proved a nasty customer had they attempted to approach the kill while he was lying there. They now hastened back to camp and arrived without further adventure.

The beaters were already assembling, but they had to be collected from a number of small villages up to a considerable distance, and it was midday before all were ready for the hunt. The procession was soon on its way to Chichkora, winding along the path through the jungle and trampling out the tracks of the past night. The beat was arranged so that the tiger might be driven up a small nullah down which he appeared to have first arrived on the scene, and up which he had dragged his prey into the thickest part of the cover filling the lower end of this nullah where it joined the main watercourse. The latter would be closed in both directions by the wings of the line of beaters. Extensive jungle stretched up the hill and over into the Shaikh Farid valley beyond, from whence the tiger had come during the night.

I was posted behind a boulder on the hillside about two hundred yards above the spot where we supposed the tiger to be lying, so as to cover a possible exit in that direction, while Robert, sitting in a low tree not more than ten feet from the ground, watched the line of the small nullah already described as his way of approach during the night and forming his probable line of retreat when driven out. No sooner had the beat begun than the clamour raised by the advancing multitude indicated that the game was afoot. Soon a great tiger, roaring fiercely, rushed out into an open glade in front of Robert, and a small boy perched in a tree twenty yards off for purposes of observation was so alarmed or excited that he tumbled from his perch into the bushes below; fortunately the beast did not see him, for Robert was so unsteady from excitement that his first bullet, fired too hastily, missed the mark; but the tiger stood still, lashing his tail; the next shot struck him full on the point of the shoulder, and dropped him dead, changed in an instant from a roaring and ferocious monster into an inert mass. Robert was delighted to have slain such a monster, exceeding in size anything we had seen or imagined, and he sat on the carcass until the beaters came up, when the tiger was slung on a small tree cut down for the purpose and sent back to camp in charge of Shaikh Karim and a dozen men to act as carriers. These would have to be used in relays to bear the burden of some four hundred and fifty pounds of dead weight on their shoulders.

We had now to decide whether to go after the tigress and cubs, said by Bhima to have killed the other buffalo at the head of Chichkora, or cross over into the Shaikh Farid valley and deal with the tiger known to be there. It is always well to consult the head shikari, whatever the extent of one's experience, and so far our experience was extremely limited. Bhima advised a move to Shaikh Farid, and to leave the tigress and cubs until next day, especially as they might have been disturbed by the sound of the distant beat, and if they had not moved, would probably be alert. This certainly seemed the wisest course, and we crossed the range of hills that lay between us and the other valley. We climbed the steep side of the hill, and emerged on to an open plateau where all the grass had been burnt in a jungle fire, and the level ground was scorched and black. Here were a few shady trees, and we were passing one of these when Bhima suddenly stopped and threw his spear with such force that it stuck quivering in the trunk of a tree. A sounder of pig, led by a good-sized boar, ran out and raced away down the rugged hillside. The spear had passed just over the boar's back. Farther on, a large blue-black antelope, a nilgai or blue bull, ran across in front of us and stood at gaze a couple of hundred yards off, offering an easy shot, but we left it alone as we did not wish to disturb the jungle, for we were now approaching the edge of the great valley. Then half a dozen nilgai cows, hornless and of a light brown or fawn colour, appeared behind their leader, and the whole herd made off, the bull leading with ungainly strides.

But now we were able to locate the kill by the

clusters of vultures that perched like foul fruit on the trees above. The tiger had evidently not left his prey, for none of the vultures descended to the ground, proof that they were afraid to approach the carcass in the presence of its guardian. The beat was quickly arranged, for the afternoon was far advanced and we could not afford delay when the tiger might be alert and about to resume his feast in the cool of the evening. The watercourse here turned towards the hills and it seemed unlikely that the tiger would attempt to break out on that side, but a driven tiger will sometimes take an unexpected course. However, he went straight up the valley and was approaching the tree behind which I stood, a large shady banyan when, being on the same level, he saw the movement as I raised my rifle, and quick as lightning turned off to one side and offered a far from easy shot as he dashed into thick cover.

When the beaters came up we went to the spot where the tiger was when fired at. The shikaris were lamenting that there was no blood on the spot and feared that it was a miss. But Nathu would not have it, and exclaimed: "We have missed no tigers!" We followed on the tracks, seeing that the tiger's claws had scored the ground; then I picked up a leaf with a spot of blood on it, and a little farther on there was more blood. We followed eagerly but with due caution, with rifles cocked and ready to fire; then Nathu exclaimed: "There is the tiger; he is dead!" There sure enough he lay dead in a small nullah. The bullet had struck him rather far back, and he had run a couple of hundred yards before dropping when he tried to climb the bank.

This tiger was a large though lanky male, about nine feet in length, only some four inches shorter than the last one. It was soon hoisted on a pole and carried off to camp for skinning. Before leaving, we went to look at the kill. The tiger had evidently seized it by the throat from below as shown by the marks of the fangs; it was lying in the open, but the vultures had not touched it; a great part of both haunches had been eaten and the tail had been bitten off and apparently swallowed as a bonne-bouche; the paunch had been removed and carefully placed at a distance; under a tree close at hand, but almost hidden by overhanging bushes, was the impression where the tiger had lain after eating his fill, and after drinking at the pool where the pugs were clearly seen in the soft mud.

At the village and camp the usual ceremonies were observed, and we saw that the red caste marks had already been put on the foreheads of the dead beasts. When the skinning began, I noticed some small punctured wounds in the back of the big tiger's neck, and remarked that he had been fighting. But when the skin was removed we saw that the punctures contained porcupine quills, and there were more quills embedded in the paws, a very common occurrence in the paws of both tigers and panthers. But this tiger must not only have killed and eaten a porcupine, but rolled on it, or how otherwise could the quills have got into the back of his neck. Chandru, having much strange lore about wild beasts, declared that the porcupine shot his quills at the tiger like arrows from a bow. Nathu agreed, and recalled how a goat picketed as bait at night for a panther was found dead in the morning with several quills embedded in its body and one at least piercing the heart. I said this was pure accident, and that the porcupine, a nocturnal animal, had come round a corner of the place in which the goat was tied up and had collided with it. Porcupines when dug out of their dens have been known to charge backwards violently at both people and dogs, so in this instance the animal may have been aggressive. Aristotle mentions the bow and arrow belief, as does Pliny in writing of both Indian and African porcupines which, he says, stretch their skins and dart forth their quills. Marlowe alludes to it in *Edward the Second*:

> Ay, ay, these words of his move me as much
> As if a goose should play the porcupine
> And dart her plumes, thinking to pierce my breast.

While the second tiger was being skinned, a long white worm was seen to exude from the cavity of the eye; no one knew anything about it or had seen such a thing before, but Chandru had suffered from a guinea-worm in his leg; the worm was wound off daily on to a stick until it had been extracted to the length of a foot or two; he declared that this worm was of the same kind.

CHAPTER X

A MIXED BAG

DURING the night a great thunderstorm arose, cooling the air and drowning the yell of jackals quarrelling over the remains of slaughtered animals; lightning flashed in the murky sky and the rain poured down in torrents. The storm gradually passed away over the hills; the moon appeared between the torn battalions of the clouds, and the echoes died away in the hills, reverberating like the rumbling thunder of distant guns whose flashes were forked lightning. Fortunately the tents were proof against the downpour and the morning broke clear and cloudless. After breakfast we started to beat up the tigress and cubs at the head of Chichkora, while a couple of men were sent to look at the buffaloes tied up across the river.

As we approached the head of the valley, a peacock uttered the trumpet note of alarm; this was taken up by another and another higher up the ravine, proving that the cause of the disturbance was on the move. Then monkeys began to chatter excitedly at the very head of the valley. No doubt the tigress and cubs were afoot. Leaving the beaters behind, we and the shikaris skirted the cover where the kill had taken place, and found the fresh tracks of the tigress and her cubs leading out towards the head of the ravine. We followed for some distance and saw that they had made off into very dense and

A MIXED BAG

extensive jungle where it was hopeless to follow them. We retraced our steps to the scene of the kill; it had been almost wholly devoured. We were not altogether disappointed, being glad that the cubs had escaped, for they were certainly not more than a year old as shown by the tracks and other indications; and had we shot the tigress it is not likely that they were old enough to look after themselves.

The question now arose what we should do, so as not to waste the remainder of the day. We thought of crossing the river to look for spotted deer, but there were some of these as well as nilgai in the valley of Chichkora, near the head of which we had now arrived. So we agreed to begin with a beat for peafowl and afterwards we could act according to circumstances and the evidences of the presence of other game, while at the same time we would avoid disturbing the jungle where we hoped to find tigers on the other bank of the river.

We beat a considerable extent of cover where there was plenty of water, posting ourselves in a fairly open line, while the beaters came along tapping the trees with their sticks and axes, and occasionally shouting. Soon the peafowl began to come out; several cocks rose in noisy flight and flew over our heads, and some half-dozen were brought to bag, as well as a few painted francolin. The beaters were than sent back to their villages after being drawn up in line and paid fourpence apiece, a little enough reward for men employed for a day in driving a dangerous wild beast from its lair. We were glad of the peafowl for the larder, although an old peacock in full plumage is a tough bird; but the chicks are excellent, equal to a pheasant. In this part of India there were no scruples about shooting these fine birds; they are much harried by native shikaris, and are in consequence wily and difficult to approach. But in Guzerat and elsewhere they are regarded as sacred by Hindus, and should, therefore, not be molested; moreover, in such protected localities they are so tame that they would in any case afford no sport.

It was now the hottest part of the day and we were glad to rest in a grove of mohwa trees whose yellow fleshy blossoms exhaled a sweet and somewhat sickly smell and were scattered in profusion on the ground. These trees have a scanty foliage of varied green and crimson hues in the month of March when the blossom ripens. The fleshy flower is disagreeable to the European palate, while their scent diffuses a peculiar fragrance for some distance and the tainted air enables one to detect the presence of the tree before it is seen. But to the human inhabitants and the beasts of the field the blossom is as the manna that fell from above, especially in years of famine when it and other jungle fruits seem providentially to blossom in more than ordinary profusion. The people flock daily to collect the fallen blossoms of this precious tree, trooping off before daybreak to the forest, bearing small baskets for carrying off the spoil.

The blossoms are used in various ways. They are dried in the sun and eaten in a natural state, and an intoxicating liquor is distilled from them. In all the hamlets in the forest in the month of March they can be seen spread out to dry on the ground outside the huts. Animals both wild and domesticated flock to the trees in great numbers; bears, nilgai, gazelle, four-horned antelope, barking-deer, and other creatures may all be looked for while they are feasting on the fallen fruit; and in the great jungles bison, sambar, and spotted deer join in the feast. Monkeys,

A MIXED BAG

the grey langur and the little brown macaque, each female now clasping her child to her breast, gather their share of the luscious blossoms, whilst birds of many species take their portion and innumerable insects add to the busy hum of life.

After resting under these trees until nearly three o'clock, we climbed the heights above to look for game. All the surviving buffalo calves had been withdrawn from the valleys, so there was no reason why game should not be hunted now that there were no tigers on the hither side of the river to be disturbed. We had not gone far when a big blue bull, looking quite black in the shade of a tree, was seen a hundred yards off. Robert knocked it over with a bullet behind the shoulder. He then ran up to it with the Subadar who drew his hunting-knife to cut the beast's throat and so make it lawful meat for Moslems; he had partly severed the windpipe when the bull struggled to its feet and made off, the blood-letting having evidently relieved it from immediate suffocation, for it was shot through the lungs. The poor animal ran half a mile before Robert brought it down with another shot.

It was a queer-looking beast, something between a cow and a horse, with its smooth short horns, horse-like neck from which depended a tassel of hair, and its ungainly action. The nilgai has often been compared with a Noah's Ark animal made of wood, such as delighted us in our childhood before the coming of mechanical and other elaborate toys. It bears a resemblance to some African species and is the largest Indian antelope, while the Hindus in some parts regard it as an ox and therefore treat it with the veneration accorded to that sacred animal. It has sometimes been said to be aggressive and dangerous, but there seems no reason for attributing this character to a mild-tempered animal. However, it is well to keep away from the heels of a wounded nilgai, as it can administer a severe kick with its strong legs and sharp-edged hoofs.

A couple of men were left to skin the nilgai and bring in the head and pelt, and later the villagers, who had no prejudices in this part of the country, went out to get the meat, a welcome supply for camp and the surrounding hamlets, while the tongue and marrow bones were set aside for our own larder. We went on our way, covering a considerable extent of country and at times descending to the nullahs to examine the water-holes. No fresh tracks of tigers were seen. Towards evening we reached a rocky height overlooking the river and the camp on one side and rising precipitously above the Shaikh Farid kora on the other. "There must be bears here," I said, pointing to a large ant-hill at least four feet high and of pyramidal form, crowned by several smaller pyramids like the minarets of a mosque. One side of the ant-hill had been scooped out and fresh marks where the bear's claws had been used to excavate it were to be seen in the hard dry earth. Bears love ants and their eggs, which they lick up with their long tongues, while their addiction to honey takes them up the trunks of trees where bees make their combs. Close by was a tall pipal tree with scratches in fives all the way up the trunk to the remains of the honeycombs.

At this season of the year the bears have a fine time, for the wild mangoes were also ripening in the forests. We went to the edge of the cliff and looked out across the broad valley, where the tops of the trees appeared like a variegated carpet below us—the mohwa, the pipal, the ebony, and the teak bereft of broad leaves that lay withered on the ground, the scarlet blossoms of the Gold Mohur tree and bright red tongues of the Flame of the Forest relieving the sea of green and yellow with splashes as of fire. The forest stretched away across the valley and climbed up the distant hill where the shrine gleamed white upon the cliff. The graceful fronds of bamboos bent and rustled in a fugitive breeze that swept across the vale and died away in gloomy thickets. Beyond again the hills rose tier upon tier, forming a gigantic amphitheatre, and the grey walls of an old fort crowned a lofty peak.

While we were contemplating this varied scene, a slight noise was heard a little way down the hill and a stone, displaced from the slope, bounded from rock to rock and plunged into the leafy depths below. " A bear! A bear! " I exclaimed, detecting a black and hairy hide visible now and then among the bushes. Following down the steep hillside, we found a little muddy water in a hollow where the bear had been scratching at a spring, now almost dry. Soon the animal appeared in an open glade far below for a moment, and was then lost to sight in dense under-growth where it was hopeless to penetrate at so late an hour. The sun was already sinking, twilight was short where night falls with sudden swiftness, and it would very soon be dark. Camp was not far distant and we could return to the hill-top in the early morning, when there would be more chance of coming to terms with the bears before those nocturnal animals, impatient of sun and heat, had retired to rest for the day. Descending the hill, we were suddenly startled by a rush of animals as a sounder of pig broke from cover and streamed away across the open, rustling through the leaves like wind. Robert raised his rifle and shot the leading boar, much to the delight of Bhima and the shikaris, who preferred pork to all other flesh; although the Moslems regarded the unclean beast with disgust. We would not shoot wild boar in a pig-sticking country, but in these vast jungles that sport is impossible; pig could not be ridden with the spear, and there was no harm in shooting them for those followers who so greatly appreciated the meat.

It was dusk when we reached camp, but the day's sport was not yet over. The headman of the village came forward after taking off his shoes, for it would be impolite of him to approach unless unshod; he bowed to the ground, at the same time making a movement with his hands as though humbly throwing dust upon his head.

"Your honour," he said, pointing to a bare hillside about half a mile off, " a panther has killed one of my calves close to the hill."

"When did this happen; is much of it eaten?" I asked.

"Last night; little has been eaten; the herdsman did not find it until your honour had gone, and he then covered the carcass to keep it from the sight of the vultures. I have had an ambush made against the hillside where your honour can shoot the robber."

There was no occasion for haste, so we agreed to dine first. Accompanied by the Subadar, we set out immediately after dinner, taking a gun with some cartridges loaded with black powder and buckshot, in addition to our rifles and water-bottles. Arrived on the scene of the tragedy, we found the body of the calf lying beside a cattle-track that led round the hill. The carcass was already unpleasant, but that did not trouble us. A space had been hollowed out in the hillside some ten or twelve feet from the kill, and a screen of thorny bushes and branches had been built in front of it with an aperture in the middle to shoot through. There was just enough space for the three of us, and we agreed that I should have the first shot and should therefore sit with the shot-gun on my knees, the other two being one on each side of me. In case the first shot was not fully effective, we could stand up and fire over the top of the screen. It was arranged that people from the camp should come after hearing a shot and a whistle-call to signify that it was safe to approach. It would not do for anyone to come if a wounded panther were about.

It may be thought somewhat unsporting to shoot with buckshot, but a panther is almost as much vermin as game, especially one that was so destructive to domesticated animals, although it is a fine beast possessing a beautiful coat and affording very good sport when beaten out and shot in daylight. But at night, even in moonlight, shooting with a rifle is very uncertain. The panther comes and goes with almost incredible swiftness, so silently and so inconspicuous, that it looks grey in the light of the moon and has been likened to a puff of smoke. This particular animal, characterised by the headman as a robber, had done much damage, killing many of the village cattle, valuable cows as well as calves and goats. A single bullet might easily miss, and a charge of buckshot at short range would be more certainly effective.

We quickly settled down behind the screen, Robert and the Subadar holding their rifles while I laid the shot-gun across my knees. The moon shone with a light almost as clear as day; for some time nothing happened; then we heard a jackal call with the " phiaou " note signifying the presence of some beast of prey, or of something that alarmed him. This jackal, or another one, shortly afterwards approached the kill and was frightened off by a stone thrown by the Subadar, who had provided himself with this ammunition for the purpose. Then a grey shadow came near with ungainly gait, and began to nose the carcass; its shape revealed its nature and it was driven off in the same manner, for we had been warned that although the panther would drive away jackals, it might be afraid to approach if a hyena was on the spot. Now we heard not far off the harsh, grating cry of the panther, and all at once it was there, having come unseen, unheard, as mysteriously as a phantom, like a cloud passing across the face of the moon. It was suddenly there behind the carcass of its victim, which moved as the beast tugged at it with his teeth. I even thought for a moment that I could smell its foul breath. It seemed to be looking straight at me, and I could see the jaws moving while they masticated the flesh, while its round head appeared over the kill. Its eyes were not glowing in the dark, as they are often represented, but the eyes themselves do not hold the light, and cannot therefore be detected in the dark, but they shine with the reflected effulgence of the moon or of a lamp or other flame.

The panther then peered in my direction, chewing a piece of flesh torn from the carcass, with its paws resting on the body, and as it seemed to be looking into my eyes I remained still until the head was again bent down to tear off another morsel; I then brought the gun slowly into position, the muzzle through the aperture, my finger on the trigger. Soon the animal again raised its head, and at once received the charge of buckshot. The smoke obscured the scene and for an instant we wondered whether there had been a miss, for we had at once sprung to our feet with our rifles ready, and even when the air cleared we could at first see nothing. Then we saw the beast's tail convulsively beating the ground, the body being hidden where it had fallen behind the dead calf.

The tail lay still after a final shudder, and we saw that all life was gone. We went out to inspect our prize, a fine male nearly seven feet long, and I blew my whistle. In ten minutes lights appeared and Nathu came up with two men who carried the dead panther back to camp in triumph, much to the delight of the whole village which had suffered so much from its depredations. The skin was soon stripped off and by midnight all was quiet and all slept in the moonlight or in the shadow of the trees. We found that the shot had struck the panther in the side of the head; the pellets were well grouped, all being covered by one hand; they had penetrated the brain, thus knocking out the animal at once.

Buckshot cartridges should always be loaded with black powder, for the large shot are not propelled with proper velocity by smokeless explosive. An officer using cartridges wrongly loaded was mortally wounded by a panther; he had fired a charge of buckshot with smokeless powder, and was attacked and badly mauled when following the beast up. It was afterwards killed, when it was found that the shot had merely penetrated the skin.

CHAPTER XI

THE EMPIRE OF NATURE

IT has been related that no buffaloes remained picketed out in Shaikh Farid and Chichkora, where we had killed the tigers on the hither side of the river. No further tracks were to be found in that part of the neighbourhood, for the tigress and cubs had apparently made off to distant jungles. There were probably no more tigers for, although these animals wander extensively during the rainy season and the cold weather, by the time the hot season sets in they have mostly settled down in certain areas where conditions with regard to food, water, and cover suit their habits. It is often said that when one tiger is killed, another will take its place at once. That is by no means the case. I have twice shot from thirteen to fourteen tigers during expeditions lasting six weeks each in particular tracts of country. On my return journeys from these two expeditions, after having practically denuded the country of the tigers it contained, I have in no instance found the places where they were killed reoccupied at the end of the six weeks. But no doubt many localities are reoccupied by the next hot weather a year later, by tigers that have wandered during the succeeding cold and rainy seasons, for such localities in the first instance were suitable in all respects for the abode of these great beasts.

THE EMPIRE OF NATURE

Two buffaloes still remained picketed in the forest across the river. But these were not enough. In order to bring to bag a large number of tigers in a limited time, it is necessary to have baits in many places covering a wide area. With a few mounted men it is not difficult to arrange this. A party with Chandru and a couple of local shikaris, as well as two of our mounted men, who had ponies bought in the bazaars for twenty or thirty rupees apiece, was accordingly sent on ten miles down the river to the next camping ground to prospect for tigers and tie up calves in likely spots where tracks were found. We would move to this spot in a couple of days' time, so this party started at daybreak on the morning after the death of the panther. At the same time a man on camel-back was sent to the post office thirty miles off to bring in our letters and papers and some supplies for the men.

We started before the sun rose and climbed the hill where the bear had been seen the previous evening, leaving Bhima with some of his villagers to inspect the calves picketed in the forest across the river. The moon had not gone down when we, together with Nathu and a couple of Banjaras, reached the top of the hill. Banjaras, who have been described as the gypsies of India owing to their having the same wandering habits of life, are especially good for this work of prospecting or watching for game and as beaters for sport of every kind. Brave and intelligent, they are a manly and in most respects a trustworthy people. They are nomadic, their homes being wherever they pitch their tents. They are to be met with in all parts of India, and before the days of railways the carrying trade of the country was largely in their hands. They were especially useful in collecting and transporting the supply of grain for armies in the field, and have figured in this capacity in all the campaigns in India during the past six hundred years. They are frequently mentioned and their services are fully described in the Despatches of the Duke of Wellington, who made use of them in the Mysore and Maratha wars.

As beaters and shikaris they are unsurpassed. Armed with spears and with the aid of a particularly fierce breed of dog, they hunt down pigs and other animals. Few carry fire-arms, but they are wonderfully skilful in knocking over small game with sticks and stones, and will even bring down running hares and birds on the wing by this means, whilst their sharp eyes enable them to detect crouching game, and so to catch hares in bushes and to kill even partridges and quail before they rise.

The sun rose and dispersed the shadows and mists of night, and as day dawned our party, distributed round the verge of the mountain, kept a sharp look-out for bears, likely to be on the move when returning to their lairs after nocturnal visits to the mohwa and mango trees in the valley below. These black sloth bears are impatient of heat, retiring at sunrise in the hot weather, although they may be found abroad some hours later during the cold season. They are found all over peninsular India, essentially an animal of the plains and lower hills, and are unmistakable with their long snout, projecting rubber lips, and the white horse-shoe mark on the chest characteristic of most species of bear. They are at times fierce and will often charge at sight, especially when come upon suddenly at close quarters. A villager with our party exhibited long claw-marks, his head looking as though it had been gone over with a garden rake, inflicted by one of these animals

CHANDRU AND NATHU, SHIKARIS.
Faithful friends and followers.

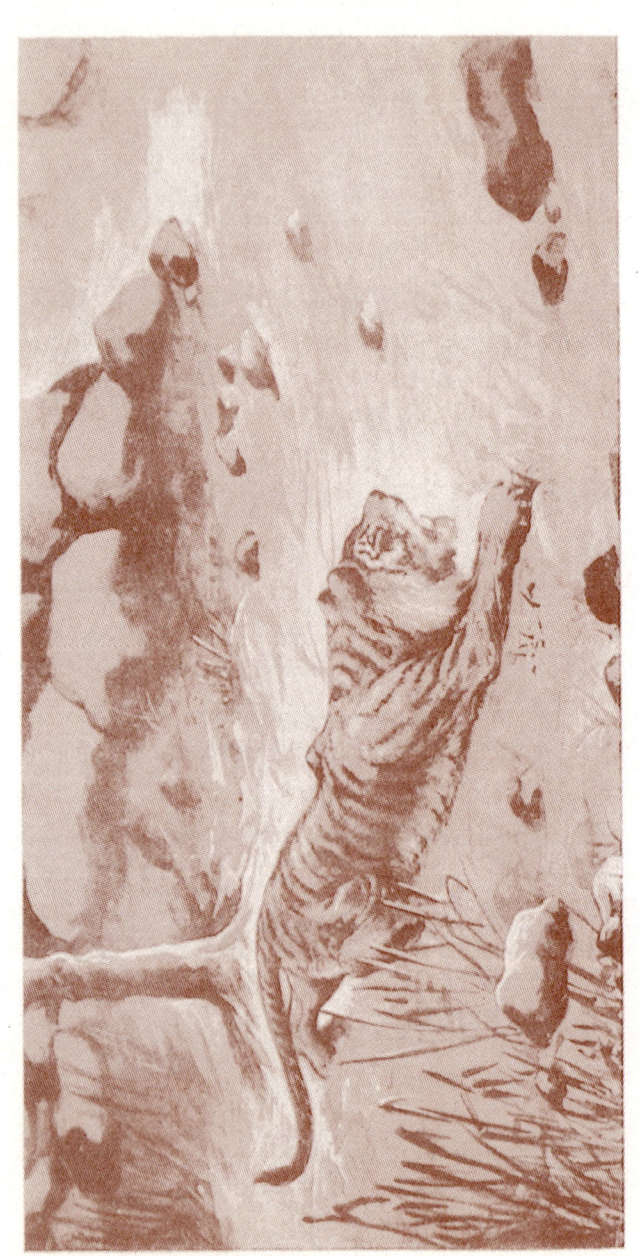

A TIGER IN THE BEAT.
Shining like molten gold in the light of the sun.

he had stumbled on when going into the forest to cut wood.

The sun was just coming up above the hills when there was a sharp whistle, in imitation of a common bird, from the Banjara naik or chief, who was sitting on a rock overlooking the Shaikh Farid kora in the direction of the ziarat. When we looked towards him he did not speak, but, holding up two fingers, pointed to the jungle below. We hurried to the spot, when he said that a bear and cub had entered a patch of grass not far below us. We climbed down the hill, and suddenly the old bear rushed out straight at us, followed by a cub about the size of a retriever dog. Robert stepped back and shot the old bear as she was passing at three or four yards' distance; the cub ran on, bumped against the naik, and scattered the men behind, scoring Nathu's leg with its sharp claws, when a Banjara with a blow from his axe cleft the skull of the plucky little beast. The shooting disturbed two other bears seen climbing the hill about one hundred and fifty yards off; I at once opened fire and at my second shot one came rolling down the hill; at the bottom its dying squeals were soon heard in a patch of bushes where it shortly expired.

I thought one of my shots had hit the other one, for it stumbled and winced but ran on. We followed on the tracks or rather in the direction it had taken, keeping as far as possible above the cover towards which it was evidently making when last seen, for it is dangerous to get below a bear or to fire at it from below; it is very likely to roll or rush down on to you with terrific impetus and a rapidity of progress that belies its name, being anything but slothful in movement. We followed on the tracks for some distance when the naik pointed here and there to a displaced stone seen to be freshly moved, from its appearance and sometimes from insects scuttling away, showing that we were close behind the animal; a scratch on hard ground or even on a rock was enough to indicate the trail. Then we found a spot of fresh blood on a stone, and a little farther on the bear had entered a patch of long grass; I passed my hand through it and withdrew it incarnadined with blood, seen on both sides of the track through the grass, thus indicating that the bullet had passed right through the bear's body. Just then there was a sudden commotion ahead and the bear rushed out open-mouthed, uttering gruff growls; a shot from my rifle dropped it dead with a bullet just over the ear.

It was now time to return to camp in case there should be a kill in the forest across the river. Leaving men to skin the bears, we went straight back to our tents and were at breakfast at ten o'clock when a man on horseback arrived with news that the first calf picketed near the pool under the great tree had been killed by a big tiger whose tracks showed that he had approached the spot from the river bank. He had not returned the same way, nor was the buffalo higher up the river killed, so it seemed almost certain that the tiger was lying up close to his prey, a place he was not likely to leave, for there was ample provision of shade and water. The area to be beaten was of limited extent, the surrounding forest being comparatively open except for a patch of heavy jungle where the tiger might be lying near his kill; or he might be in the water or in the open under the tree where he would have the benefit of any breeze that blew.

Tigers are impatient of heat and thirst, one of the reasons generally adduced for the theory that they have migrated into India from the cradle of the race within the Arctic circle, where their bones are found in pleistocene deposits together with those of other still existent animals, no doubt driven to more temperate climates by the advancing ice-cap, the tiger following its prey before the onset of those frozen solitudes. Another reason for this supposition is that they are not found in Ceylon, an island separated from the mainland of the peninsula within recent geological time. However, tigers are found in Malaya, including the islands of Java, Sumatra, and Bali. They are often spoken of in literature relating to Gautama Buddha, and seals bearing representations of them have been dug up in the ruins of the ancient city of Mohenjo Daru in the valley of the Indus, dating from 5000 years back, so migration into sub-tropical regions must have taken place many centuries ago. As for impatience of heat, that applies to all animals and even birds in hot climates.

In ground like that where this tiger was lying, few beaters are wanted, and thirty men collected in the village near our camp, in addition to our own following, were considered enough. We walked to the point of assembly where the beat was to be arranged, and it did not take long to post the few stops required and take up our own positions. At the first shout of the beaters a herd of spotted deer, led by a fine stag, trotted out close to me, but I, of course, did not shoot the stag for fear of turning the tiger. He soon gave evidence of his presence by angry roars on one flank of the beat, where a wing led by Nathu was advancing through bush cover. Here he was driven back, and I heard Nathu's voice abusing the tiger and telling him to get along and be shot. The beast turned back, and with an angry grunt trotted through the jungle straight towards me, leaping lightly into a hollow in the ground in front of me. There he stopped, turning his head in the direction of the beat and listening to the noise that pursued him.

A bullet behind the shoulder made him spring forward with a fierce growl, but another stretched him out and he lay gasping horribly, at times half raising himself and falling back again with the bloody foam from his lungs frothing on his jaws. Another bullet was required to finish him off. This was a short tiger, nine feet in length, but very fat and heavy, having no doubt fed well on the deer abounding in the forest and varying his diet occasionally by carrying off cattle from the neighbourhood of the riverside villages, and at times attacking stray ones from the herds that were driven down to water and to crop the fresh grass on the bank of the stream. On these occasions, the herdsmen told us, they seldom had a glimpse of him, for he would not take an animal out of the herd when the herdsman was watching his charges; he would follow generally on the way to the village in the evening, keeping under cover and picking up any straggler that might loiter behind. Indeed this remarkable timidity on the part of a mighty carnivorous animal possessing such terrible strength and armature is a most noteworthy feature in the character of the tiger and leopard. It seems probable, however, that it is not due to fear or timidity, but to the natural habit of the beast in cautious approach to its wild prey, necessary to ensure success in securing its food.

Old Brook Sahib had come up with another calf to be picketed in place of the deceased, whose remains were carried off by the low-caste people for the sake of the beef they did not wish to relinquish to jackals and vultures. The tiger was skinned on the spot, the head being taken back to camp by my old herdsman, who was soon employed in cleaning the skull added to the collection surrounding his lair under the cart.

It was now past one o'clock, and we rested for a time in the shade of the trees on the river bank. Here it was comparatively cool and pleasant, while our surroundings were beautiful and interesting. Great trees dotted with the nests of vultures stood upon the banks where they must have grown, and where the birds no doubt had made their homes for hundreds of years. The forest was dry and in places burnt, but on the margin of the watercourse the verdure kept green by moisture was a relief to the eye. Thick cane brakes and tall elephant grass afforded a retreat for many creatures, while clumps of bamboo and teak and other trees filled the level ground and climbed up the hills. Shady nullahs, containing here and there a pool of water, joined the river at frequent intervals. In the forest was an infinite variety of wild life, now silent and at rest during the heat of the day. To the lover of nature there could be no greater pleasure on earth than to wander over these far solitudes.

Our talk turned on the events of the morning, and Nathu was praised for his boldness in turning back the tiger when it attempted to break out of the beat. He described how he had faced the animal when it was angry and stood roaring at him and lashing its tail, and how he had driven it single-handed on to the guns when it attempted to escape.

" That was very well done, Nathu, but we don't want you to be killed," I said.

" What of that, sahib," replied the old man, " we

can but die once, and the tiger is a splendid beast; and if I am killed it will be my fate."

Bhima, who never lost a chance of chaffing Nathu in a friendly way, joined in, saying: "But perhaps you will be killed by a bear, like that cub which scratched you this morning."

But Nathu gave as good as he got: "No inferior animal will kill me," he said; "look at my face which was clawed by a panther; it would be a fine death to be killed by a tiger, the raja of all the beasts of the forest."

"Take care that hyena does not catch you; it was prowling about the camp last night after visiting the panther's kill," remarked Bhima, determined to have the last word.

"Yes," retorted Nathu, "I expect it got your scent, Bhima; and I hope you will be careful not to be caught by a crocodile while crossing the river."

It was now three o'clock and we decided to follow the course of the river in search of more game. More than one herd of spotted deer was seen, but they were not molested as we did not at present wish to kill these beautiful animals, while we were also in the vicinity of prospective tiger-beats. We had gone about half a mile when Bhima pointed out some crocodiles lying on a sandbank where they were basking in the sun, fast asleep with their mouths wide open while little birds hopped in and out of their gaping jaws, catching insects or picking the reptiles' teeth. We each selected a crocodile and fired at the same instant; one about nine feet long lay kicking convulsively on the sand while the other made off into the river where it sank in the crimsoned stream, evidently hit. But it had disappeared, and if dead would not be expected to come to the surface for several days.

The dead crocodile, whose convulsions had now ended, was soon stripped of the skin of its belly and the underneath part of its legs, the only portions useful for tanning into leather. It was then cut open, when a strange assortment of articles was found in the stomach; these comprised a silver bracelet, a two-anna piece, a small silver coin, a number of pebbles swallowed to aid digestion, and the carcass of a wild cat. I remarked to Bhima that it must have killed and eaten someone, as no one would part with the bracelet and coin except with his life, a sly dig at the proclivities of his kind which the shikari fully appreciated.

"Yes," he replied, "that may be so; but some unfortunate person may have been drowned, and there is a burning ghat where the bodies of the dead are burnt a little farther down the river."

We now turned a bend of the river and saw on the water's edge a funeral pyre on which a corpse was burning, the blue smoke ascending into the ambient air. The mourners, having set fire to the wood, were just leaving the scene, and as we came near the pyre fell in, the half-burned corpse subsided amid the ashes, and the skull went off with a pop like the bursting of a paper bag. This served as a dinner bell for the hungry monsters lurking in the river on the look-out for prey. A horrible scene followed. Suddenly from the water rushed four or five immense turtles; they seized and tugged at the remains, running back to the river with limbs and other portions in their jaws. Heedless of the burning wood and heat, they pulled at their prey, while the glowing embers scorched them so that the skin could be seen curling upon their backs. Then the flames shot up again, licking the reptiles and driving them back into the river to quench the fires that scorched them; soon the flames died down, the fire smouldered, while more turtles came out of the river to get their share of this foul food.

We hurried from this scene and crossed the river a mile farther on, where there was a small impoverished hamlet inhabited by Sikhs. They presented a wretched and ragged appearance, far different from those members of their martial race and militant community whom we meet in more prosperous circumstances in our Army and elsewhere. Yet the distinctive characters of their race were distinguishable in their features and bearing, notwithstanding their unkempt appearance. They said that their colony had been established at the time of the great Mutiny in 1857, perhaps by offenders fleeing from justice and taking refuge to this remote and unfrequented spot.

CHAPTER XII

DESTROYERS IN THE FOREST

IN the forests of India death is ever at work both by day and by night. The fierce tiger slinks to his lair at dawn of day, noiselessly stalking with velvet footfall in the shady places of the forest accompanied by the bark of the deer, the cry of the peafowl, and the chattering of monkeys. In the cooler seasons of the year he may hunt also by day, but he is impatient of heat and in summer seldom stirs abroad after the sun is well up in the heavens, preferring to lie in the shade or in a pool of water. The panther is also essentially a nocturnal animal, prowling round jungle hamlets to pick up dogs and goats, or in more secluded haunts killing small deer, wild pigs, antelope, monkeys, and peafowl. Of other great carnivora the bear can scarcely be termed a destroyer, for he seldom molests animals and is generally content with a diet of roots and insects. The hyena is more of a scavenger, though partial to dogs, and has been known to carry off children.

The hunting leopard lives mainly on antelope, and the red lynx or caracal preys on smaller animals and birds; but these two, both of which in captivity are used in the chase, are seldom met with by the sportsman, for they are rare animals. The wild dog is perhaps more rapacious than all; a pack of these vermin will rapidly denude a country of game, and even the tiger and panther have at times been attacked by them. The wolf is found in more open country where antelope, sheep, goats, and dogs afford him a good living, while he is responsible for the death of many human beings. Then there are jackals, foxes, civets, martens, a host of lesser cats, and many snakes that add to the list of destroyers.

In the stillness of the night the moon shone down upon the scene, flooding all the open spaces with its soft effulgence, outlining the trees which spectral-like stretched their branches bare of leaves to the cool night air. But the great tree over the pool in the jungle covered with deep shadow the water beneath, where one solitary star was reflected peeping through the leafy canopy above. On the brink of the pool the tethered buffalo calf stood chewing the cud, all unconscious of the striped destroyer approaching from the river bank. Twenty yards off, the skeleton of the slain tiger, picked clean by vultures, lay white and ghastly with crimson streaks in the bright light of the moon. A fugitive breeze stirred the dry leaves and passed on to die in the thickets at the foot of the adjacent hill. The buffalo looked up, turned in the direction from whence the breeze had come and stood at gaze.

Perhaps he scented danger; the midnight air might well have brought him a taint of impending doom, for from the same direction a great beast of prey, grey in the moonlight, passed almost like a shadow from glade to glade. It paused for a moment motionless on the bank of the nullah, a thing of terror yet of splendour. The buffalo moved, stamped his hoof, and then bent down to get a mouthful of grass, and the tiger instantly crouched, watching the unconscious beast that stood chewing the cud. Then he approached behind the shelter of a bush and from a few yards' distance rushed upon his prey. With his paws and extended claws he seized the beast round the neck and shoulder, his jaws closed on the back of the neck, he tugged and turned his victim over and as it fell the neck was broken.

The tiger dropped his prey for a moment and then again seized it and with a wrench broke the rope that tethered it by the foreleg. He did not suck the blood from the jugular vein ; he picked up the calf as a cat picks up a mouse, and with the hind-legs dragging and leaving a trail along the ground, he walked off towards a patch of bush. He came to the spot where lay the skeleton of his luckless predecessor, shot the day before, and dropped his burden. He sniffed at the remains, turned, and fled like a spectre into the depths of the forest, reached the river bank, and went away across a stretch of sand, making for some distant haunt.

Meanwhile another tragedy was being enacted higher up the watercourse at the place where the second buffalo was picketed, and a more unusual one than that just described. A great bull bison came down to the water to drink, for here too a little moisture had as yet not been dried up by the heat of the summer sun. As he approached the pool he saw the wretched beast tied up there and stood for a time gazing at this unusual intruder. He stamped his hoofs, snorted, pawed up the ground, apparently filled with sudden rage, as a bull bison behaves when drinking near a tiger's kill. Then he rushed upon the tethered animal, gored it with his massive pointed horns, trampled on it with all his great weight, and did not desist until it lay inert and lifeless ; then seemingly satisfied with his work, the great beast drank his fill at the pool and departed slowly into the shadows of the forest. The story of this night's happenings was plainly seen in the marks on the ground.

At seven o'clock next morning we started for the forest across the river. From a distance we observed the buffalo under the big tree by the pool and at once saw that it was dead. But examination through the binoculars disclosed that none of the carcass had been eaten. This seemed curious, but the tiger may have been feeding well and not wanted to eat again yet; he might be lying close by, although we could not see him; but a tiger is rarely visible in such circumstances. We found tracks made on his approach and other tracks leading away towards the bank of the river. We followed these as far as possible and saw that without doubt the tiger had made off. His tracks were on a sand bank down to the stream and there he had crossed to the other side where the water was shallow; and sometimes galloping, as was evident from the impressions of his paws, had fled to distant haunts. The shikaris declared that the ghost of the dead tiger haunted the spot and warned other tigers of their danger.

We now went on to look at the other buffalo higher up the watercourse, and discovered the havoc wrought by the bison; thus the story of two extraordinary incidents was written in the book of Nature in tracks and other signs during one night as already described. Bison were protected in this part of the country as their numbers had been greatly reduced by an epidemic of foot-and-mouth disease; there was, therefore, no object in pursuing this ferocious bull, so we continued on our way up the nullah. Here near another pool we found tracks of a tiger, apparently the same animal, for the measurements corresponded with those of the footprints near the kill, although they were two days old, so Bhima

DESTROYERS IN THE FOREST

said. Certainly they were not at all clear-cut like those of the night. The tiger had eaten a number of crabs whose remains were scattered in the water and on the brink : still more curious was a large python bitten in two and fished out of the pool on the point of Bhima's spear. The tiger had bitten a large piece out of its middle, but apparently not caring for the taste of it he had flung the remains into the water.

Continuing on our way we saw a large blue bull feeding on the tender shoots of the bamboo, and with a good shot Robert dropped it dead with a bullet behind the shoulder. Leaving men to skin and cut up the animal, we turned homewards at this point, promising to send out villagers to help with the blue bull ; they would cut up the whole carcass and hang strips of flesh on trees and bushes to dry for future use. We had many preparations to make for our departure on the following morning ; these occupied the rest of the day ; before nightfall the tents were struck, and everything was packed up and loaded on bullock carts ready for the journey. Only our beds and materials for breakfast were left unpacked.

Before daybreak we mounted our horses and rode along the path that followed the river bank on the way to the next camping ground. The river, winding with serpentine course for many a mile, was beautiful in the early morning. Spotted deer were to be seen in herds along the bank, while gorgeous peacocks with their sober-plumaged hens scuttled to cover on our approach. From the water great storks and herons rose and flapped off on lazy pinions. Gazelle abounded in the fields that stretched from the foot of the hills to the water's edge, and four-horned antelope appeared in the glades of the forest on the farther bank of the river. In the trees we saw large rufous-coloured squirrels, nearly three feet in length, the tail longer than the body. There were also numbers of Imperial pigeons, immense birds uttering their booming notes, sitting on the tops of the tallest trees.

We sat down on the river bank at eleven o'clock for our luncheon from a basket carried by a villager, and as there was no need to hurry we remained some time on this beautiful spot to enjoy the scenery and the sights and sounds of the jungle. We hoped for news of a kill at the new camping-ground, but there was no object in getting there long before beaters had been assembled. At noon we dismounted in a grove of trees near a hamlet where we were met by the Subadar and Chandru with news of a kill not far off, but no tracks of tigers were found and it was probable that we had to deal with a panther. However, we reached camp to find the beaters ready and we started at once. The kill was in an extensive patch of dense jungle through which a deep and narrow ravine, beginning in a cleft in the rocks, ran down from the hills. But the hills above were bare, and it was advisable to drive the beast down towards the river bank, for no animal would break into the open country on the hills.

The jungle about the kill was very dense with tangled green, red, and yellow bush, principally korinda and lokandi, an evergreen furnishing cover throughout the year and practically impenetrable. The beat began soon after midday with some thirty peasants and our own men in line. A bevy of peafowl were at once disturbed, some flew and some ran down the ravine; an old grey boar broke away, and after a time the clamour of the beaters stopped and one of our men shouted out that a panther had gone into a thicket and refused to move. But at a given signal the beaters above this cover set up a simultaneous yell, while a shower of stones was flung into the cover and the Subadar fired a charge of small shot into the thicket. This had the desired effect; monkeys in the trees overhead chattered excitedly, springing from branch to branch, and the panther dashed out, roaring fiercely, and tore like a streak of yellow light across the narrow space in front of me, but I missed it with both barrels and it afforded no view to Robert, who was standing on the other side of the ravine. A further beat produced no result; the beast had gone clear away into heavy jungle on the river bank.

We were astonished at the number of tigers and panthers in this part of the country. But it must not be supposed that these animals are wholly pernicious. Certainly they kill valuable cattle, and it is well that we should reduce their numbers. But they have their uses in the economy of Nature, for they keep down the pig and antelope that ravage the crops unless kept within bounds. I have observed that where there are no tigers and panthers, or where these have been nearly exterminated, cultivation is sometimes almost impossible, so great is the damage done by the hog and antelope which furnish the natural prey of the great carnivora. There is another and a deeper meaning in these tragedies of Nature. The perfection, development, and even the continued existence of species depend largely on the maintenance of predaceous beasts. They are the natural means of providing for the survival of the fittest by the elimination of the weak and diseased. Otherwise these would breed and sow the seeds of the dissolution of their race. For, speaking generally, the weaklings and the unfit are the first victims of the destroyers, being more easily caught and killed and often meeting their fate before they have time to produce defective offspring.

Chandru had been sent in the morning to the hills above the village of Ambari to bring news of tigers from that favourite haunt, some five miles distant, where we afterwards shot many tigers. A man now came with news that they had found tracks of a tigress leading into a deep ravine, into which it had dragged some wild animal killed on the hill above. Chandru remained on the spot and sent word that only about twenty men would be required for the beat. Taking our shikaris and a few beaters we rode off to the place, approached by a very rough mountain track; for some miles along this we had to dismount and lead our horses. From a distance we saw vultures hovering in the sky above, and by degrees going down into the ravine; we found this to be a mere cleft in the hill. Like all these jungles, the cover was so dense that it was impossible to seek out and stalk the tiger where she lay, so with a gun on each side near the exit of the ravine we covered the probable line of retreat, while a few men placed at intervals along the brink on either side were enough to drive the beast back if she should attempt to break out up hill. The tigress gave no trouble; she came walking down the bed of the ravine soon after the beat began, and Robert, sitting on the hillside above, dropped her dead with a bullet through the heart. Then a great black bear broke through the bushes on the hillside. It trundled up to the top, and rushed close past the syces who were standing with the horses, afterwards offering a very difficult shot to Robert, but escaping unscathed. We went to view the tigress's kill and found the remains of a four-horned antelope, almost entirely devoured. This has not taken long to relate, but the place was seven miles from our camp, and it was quite dark by the time we had threaded the rocky path down the mountains and reached our tents without further adventure.

A party had been sent on to Ambari to prospect for more tigers, several being reported in the vicinity. In the morning we sent the camp up a considerable valley containing the hamlet of Ambari, where the tents were pitched under some trees a couple of miles from the village and four miles from the river. We ourselves crossed the river and entered the great forest to look for tracks of tigers and in quest of any other game worthy of the rifle. Taking as our line of advance a watercourse opposite the camp, we started at daybreak and had not gone far when a fine spotted stag crossed not forty yards in front of us; but we did not wish to shoot more of these beautiful creatures unless the necessities of the camp demanded venison, so it was left alone. After the sun was up we went over a jungle-clad spur, when suddenly a stag sambar sprang up out of long grass in which it was lying and dashed off with its head bent down and horns lying along its back. Robert brought it down with a quick shot; it proved to be a large, heavy beast with poor antlers. It was rather remarkable to find a sambar with antlers, as these are generally cast in March, much earlier than those of the spotted deer which carry their horns during the hot weather. We were glad to get this sambar, not for the sake of a worthless trophy, but for the skin to be tanned as valuable soft leather for shooting boots, while the flesh was welcome for the poor Sikhs of a village colony of these people, and for Banjaras who had an encampment in the neighbourhood. There were also many Gond hamlets whose inhabitants were dependent for sustenance mainly on the animal and vegetable products of the jungle.

After a mile or two we came to an open glade where several herds of spotted deer and some nilgai were standing quite unconcerned at our presence. There were also monkeys grey and brown, peafowl, a cow bison with two calves of different sizes and ages, and a brace of wild dogs on the far side of the glade, the latter appearing to take no notice of so many of the creatures that form their prey. The dogs, so destructive to game, could not be allowed to go in peace, so we each fired at one. The crack of the rifles had immediate effect; in a few moments every living thing disappeared except the monkeys bouncing about in the branches. One dog was obviously hit, although it followed its companion. We soon came up with and killed it with another shot. Its tail was wet with a strong-smelling ammoniac liquid; the natives believe that the dogs blind their quarry by flicking this liquid into their eyes with the tail. The red dog was a large strong male, having remarkably developed muscles and limbs, a bright rufous coat, much lighter underneath, and a black-tipped tail. It was much larger and heavier than a jackal, and we were glad to have killed so destructive an animal, for hunting in packs up to twenty or more in number, they destroy great quantities of game.

CHAPTER XIII

THE GREAT AMBARI TIGER

THE hills fall rapidly towards the jungle hamlet of Ambari which stands in a clearing in the forest. The villagers possessed a few herds of cattle, and these with the sambar and nilgai inhabiting the surrounding forest formed an attraction to the tigers in bamboo-clad valleys. There were some patches of cultivation round the village. Our camp was pitched a couple of miles off under great trees; beneath one a red-painted stone furnished the symbol of the presiding deity of this wild spot, called Ganeshpur from a village that once stood upon this ground, named after Ganesh, the elephant god.

A couple of miles from the village the valley split into two branches, one thickly overgrown with tall grass and bamboo, the other with sparse bushes, but containing more plentiful water and several cane brakes affording good cover for tigers. There were also other branches leading into the two main watercourses. In the evening the shikaris, who had started out prospecting before our arrival in camp, came in with news of several tigers, producing pieces of dry grass stalks showing measurements of the pugs. One track looks so like another that in the absence of any marked difference or unusual character it is often only by measurements that one can tell whether the tracks are made by different tigers or by one and the same animal, and whether there is more than one tiger inhabiting a particular tract of country, unless there are tigers and tigresses, the impressions of whose feet are easily distinguishable. But a very old tiger's toes are often splayed out, as the shikaris said one of these tracks indicated; they had put up this tiger in a pool of water where he was lying in the heat of the day, and they described him as a beast of immense size and faded by age to a pale colour. It is curious that the tiger is the only one of the tribe of great cats thus partial to water; in Malaya tigers used to swim across from the mainland to the island of Singapore and back again, while in the Sundarbans of the Ganges estuary they have even been known to board passing boats. The panther or leopard, on the other hand, does not readily take to water and unlike the tiger may often be found in dry country far from drinking places.

The shikaris, who it will be remembered had been sent on ahead to Ambari a day before we moved our camp to that place, had tied up half a dozen buffaloes in favourable localities, and were confident that there would be at least one kill during the first night. During the hours of darkness a great thunderstorm arose, a not infrequent occurrence in these hills during the hottest weather; the thunder reverberated among the mountains and valleys, drowning the yell of the jackals' gathered cry, while lightning flashed ever and anon in the murky sky, revealing the wild forest glade where the camp was pitched, and the rain poured down in torrents. But morning broke bright and clear and, soon after the sun was up, Bhima and I went to look at the buffaloes picketed up one branch of the valley, while Robert accompanied the Subadar and some of the shikaris up the other branch.

THE GREAT AMBARI TIGER

The rain of night glistened like diamonds on trees and grass in the rays of the morning sun; the air was fresh and sweet and the unwonted coolness had instilled fresh life into birds and beasts and flowers. We moved cautiously, fearing to disturb tigers which generally walk about in the vicinity of the kill until the heat of the sun drives them to seek the shelter of the thickets or the water, or the shadow of some giant tree whose gnarled trunk and leafy canopy shields them from the blaze of the sun. As we passed up the valley, Bhima silently pointed with his spear to the pugs of a tiger on the damp path, where the impressions looked almost as big as a soup plate or the footmark of a large camel. I measured it and found that it corresponded with the longest grass stalk.

"The biggest tiger!" whispered Bhima. The first buffalo was close at hand, but much to our surprise the animal was alive and was patiently chewing the cud. It uttered a feeble grunt. Sure enough the tiger had passed close by without molesting the bait put out to attract him. More than this, he had lain down by the pool.

"Look, sahib; he has drunk water," said Bhima, indicating the pugs on the margin of the pool. I saw the impress of the great beast's body and of his mighty paws in the soft ground only eight or ten yards from where the buffalo stood. Why he had not killed the wretched animal could only be conjectured, but Bhima had an explanation.

"Jadu!" (Sorcery) he exclaimed.

It was certainly difficult to account for. The tiger had walked swiftly away from the bank of the nullah where the buffalo was picketed and had descended into the watercourse again about half a mile farther on, where tracks showed that he was joined by a tigress. There, after the tigress had left him, he had killed another buffalo tied up to intercept his attention in case he should not have passed within reach of the first one; this proved that he had not passed by the first one from any disinclination to kill and feed.

"Doubtless the jungle god forbade him to kill the first one," said Bhima, who was always ready to feast on the sacrificial goat provided on such occasions. "We must give a goat to the god," he added, no doubt thinking also of the liquor that would accompany the feast.

I suggested that the tiger must have been alarmed by a sudden clap of thunder. But this was certainly a somewhat feeble idea, for, as Bhima remarked: "The sahib shows much wisdom, but this is an old tiger who must have heard much thunder in his time. Why, then, should he fear it?"

When we got back to camp we found that there had been a kill by a tigress. Beaters were already assembling, and by midday we started for the place about two miles off. The kill had been dragged into a dense cane brake, but we beat all the surrounding country in vain. The ground was too hard and stony to show tracks, but the tigress must have gone off to some distant haunt, probably at daybreak. This confirmed Bhima's view of *jadu* due to an offended jungle god, in one case preventing the big tiger from killing the first buffalo, and in the other warning the tigress off her kill.

However, there was still the big tiger to be hunted out, and in an hour we were on the spot and the beat was arranged. Robert and I were posted on a rock overlooking the watercourse and the beat had not proceeded far when we saw an immense tiger coming lazily up the nullah; apparently he must pass close

THE GREAT AMBARI TIGER

to us and already we counted him as ours. Suddenly a four-horned antelope came racing along the bank of the watercourse below us and jumped down right in front of the tiger. The great beast was so startled that with a growl he sprang up the steep bank of the watercourse and made off across country, getting away without offering a shot. No stop had been posted at that spot, and but for this mishap no tiger would have left the beat at such a place.

The shikaris were now convinced that the jungle god was displeased and must be propitiated if we were to have any success with wild beasts under his protection. A goat was sacrificed with the usual ceremonies in front of the red-painted stone under a tree near the tents, after it had been anointed with spirit and made to bow down before the graven image. Half a dozen bottles of daru, the ordinary country liquor, were given to the shikaris for celebrating the occasion at the feast, and all retired to rest with the firm conviction that we would have a successful day with the help of the Spirit of the Wild.

For three days nothing happened. Day after day we covered the whole country, reading in the book of nature imprinted on the ground the comings and goings of tigers in their nightly prowling in search of prey. Then the big tiger killed another buffalo and lay beside the carcass in a pool of water. We made a circuit of the spot and our first idea was to stalk the beast and get a shot at him as he lay in or emerged from the pool. But the approach was almost impossible owing to the nature of the surrounding cover and the position of the pool, precluding the probability of an undetected approach; the tiger would be disturbed and would make off without offering a chance of a shot. We therefore decided that it was best to drive him out in the usual manner. At the first shout of the beaters the tiger came along dripping with water and growling, no doubt with disgust at being disturbed from his cool siesta in the heat of the day. But when it appeared that success was assured, he turned suddenly out of the beat without apparent cause, and made off without exposing himself to a shot from either of us. We followed some miles in the direction he had taken, and beat more cover but could not find him again.

Failure only added to our determination. We cut across country for a few miles to intercept the route he had taken, and picketed several buffaloes near pools of water on his probable line of retreat, so that the whole country round the locality where he had taken up his abode was enclosed in a circle of living bait, and it was unlikely that he would make his way out without coming upon a picketed calf at the water where he would have to drink.

That night he killed another buffalo, this time only a mile from camp; the shikaris regarded this as carrying the war into the enemy's country, for they ascribed to wild beasts a human cunning and power of thought they surely do not possess. Still Bhima was confident, for, said he, the jungle *deo* has been propitiated and we shall get him this time, while Nathu added with oriental flattery: "No tiger has yet escaped the sahibs; all are shot like hares." But ill-luck, or rather bad management followed, for my own belief in luck is of the slightest. While we were arranging the beat, some of the stops, approaching too near to the spot where the beast was lying, disturbed him before we were ready; roaring angrily, the tiger made off towards the camp, and indeed passed within sight of those followers who had remained there, causing the cook to leave his pots and pans and shin up the nearest tree. The animal then took cover in a dense and extensive cane-brake not far from the tents, and when we tried to drive him out of this, he broke back roaring through the line of beaters, scattering them in all directions, and retreated towards the head of the valley where it was now too late to follow him, the hunt having occupied the whole day until darkness that so swiftly falls in the tropics was already descending upon us.

We went to look at the kill next morning when the sun was a spear's length above the hills, not expecting to find that the tiger had been bold enough to return to the part of the jungle where he had been so closely and persistently pursued. The carcass had disappeared! Cautiously approaching, we saw tracks of the night clearly imprinted on the water's edge, while the remains had been dragged into the middle of the pool by the tiger, probably to preserve it from vultures and jackals. The tracks led straight away from the pool, and we were following these when I was suddenly overcome by the sun, and collapsed with what was evidently sunstroke, choleraic symptoms and a high temperature in a few minutes reducing me to a condition of extreme weakness. I could neither walk nor mount my pony, so a bullock-cart was sent for and I was taken back to camp, jolted over the rough ground in that uncomfortable springless vehicle.

Those who have suffered from sunstroke will understand the helpless condition to which I was reduced for some days. Unable to bear the light of day, I had to remain in a darkened tent, covered over with black blankets stretched across the ridge-pole to keep out the glare of the sun. There I lay for three days unable to move, and then my temperature went down, and although still very weak I was able to get up and sit outside the tent for a short time in the evening. In the meantime the tiger killed another buffalo, but in my interests was left undisturbed in possession of his prey, chiefly in the hope that I would soon be able to take part in another hunt, and partly in order to allow the beast to quiet down and afford us another chance of driving him out and securing his destruction.

The tigress also killed two buffaloes, but it was evident that she had the habit of leaving her kill at or soon after dawn and going off to some unknown lair at a considerable distance. Two days later the big tiger killed again in the same valley, but the shikaris disturbed him when visiting the kill. I was still too weak to be exposed to the sun in the heat of day, so Robert went out accompanied by the Subadar, Bhima, Chandru, and Nathu, with a couple of men to lead a string of calves, and determined to bring to bag the beast that had wrought so much destruction and led us so long a chase.

Taking up the trail from the kill, he tracked the animal several miles into a long narrow valley we had not hitherto visited. Here a pool of water was found among the rocks and a buffalo was picketed upon the spot. Close by was dense cover, clumps of bamboo, jamun bushes, and tall grass forming ideal cover for the tiger. Every tiger has his peculiarities and this one, now known so well, seemed to be a peculiar animal apart from the water-loving propensities common to all his tribe. He appeared to have entered into the spirit of the chase, and it could be imagined that he grinned with pleasure in foiling our efforts to encompass his destruction. He dominated all the thoughts of the hunters and camp followers.

Before daybreak the shikaris and other trusty men

THE GREAT AMBARI TIGER

went out to occupy points of vantage on the ground high above the ravine, from whence, unseen themselves, they might be able to observe the tiger's movements. Dawn came, and they saw the great beast lying beside the carcass of the calf which he had killed and partly devoured during the night. The sun rose, and when the kill was no longer in the shade, the tiger, thirsty after his bloody feast, got up and entered the water, drank with lapping tongue, and then retired to lie up in the thicket close at hand. A couple of men came swiftly to camp with the news; a hundred beaters were assembled, and by midday we started, myself in a bullock-cart as I was still too weak to ride or walk. I felt confident that before nightfall the tiger would ride back to camp with me in the cart!

The whole countryside had gathered to the beat, for the fame of this great tiger, reputed to be under the special protection of the jungle god, had spread far and wide. This special dispensation of the *deo* did not imply that the people were averse from the destruction of the animal; they hoped that the deity had been propitiated by the sacrifices offered at the shrine in the forest, and that death would overtake the tiger that had harried their flocks for nearly a year. To these superstitions were added the enthusiasm of those who were anxious to deal with the beast which had led us so arduous a chase, while even my illness was ascribed to divine intervention in favour of the tiger. His immense size, enhanced by a great ruff of almost leonine proportions round his neck and jowl, his reputed ferocity, an attribute too commonly applied to all of the species, and his habit of lying in water, immersed, it was said, so that only the tip of his tail was to be seen above the surface, all these were exaggerated, while it was even rumoured in the neighbouring villages that he had gone into the tents to look for us.

People of many races assembled round our camp, eager to have a part in the chase. There were Marathas, Moslems, Bhils, Gonds, and Telingas, whilst a contingent of Sikhs, recognisable in spite of their beards being ragged and unbrushed, but bearing the fine features and presence of their race, were recruited from a hamlet on the bank of the river, where their ancestors were said to have taken refuge when driven from the Punjab. A band of Banjaras, that wandering tribe who live in tents, came from a neighbouring tanda encamped by the stream, in charge of their naik and anxious to see the sport and to earn the fourpence a head paid to the beaters.

The valley was narrow, providing space for our two guns only, one on either side. The bullock-cart carried me to the entrance to this ravine where it widened out into the main valley; here we separated, Robert going round the top on his side to get above the tiger, while I painfully and with the help of the Subadar and Bhima, climbed the rocky steep and got to the top with difficulty, overlooking the spot where, all unconscious of his impending fate and gorged with the fat of many oxen, the great tiger was taking his midday siesta in a thicket. We followed the crest of the ravine, posting a few stops, and disturbing an almost unnoticed bear among the rocks half way; he trundled off over the ridge, an insignificant animal compared with the prospective tiger. Then we climbed down into the glen opposite the place where Robert was posted, half a mile beyond the cover where the tiger lay, and where the heights on either side narrowed in to form a boulder-strewn gorge of open ground just beyond a dense bamboo ticket. Here, in a somewhat exhausted condition, for the climb both up and down had been somewhat stiff, I sat on the ground beside a boulder which afforded some concealment. The two guns thus covered the whole of the ground over which the tiger was likely to retreat before the advancing beat, although each had in front of him an open space shut off between the two, by scattered rocks and bushes, and thus obscured from the view of the other.

The Subadar and Bhima, from the one side, and Chandru and Nathu from the other side, where they had been posting stops, rejoined the beaters, the main body of whom had been assembled at the entrance to the ravine, while the Banjaras formed a line on one side of the heights and a large party was lined on the other flank. All was now ready and the fate of the beast seemed to be assured.

It is not always wise to have too much noise in the beat, for this may cause the tiger to gallop or to break out on one flank or the other. But if there is not enough noise, the beaters may come too suddenly on the beast at close quarters, for he is generally somnolent during the heat of the day and is not always easily roused, and he may break back, perhaps injuring someone in the process. The reputation of this animal had inspired the peasants with some dread. On a given signal they advanced, sending forth a simultaneous uproar and continuing to shout as they ascended the ravine, while the lines forming the flanks on the heights moved silently, conforming to the movements of the main body of beaters.

The tiger soon gave notice of his presence, taking the unusual course of ascending the side of the ravine over the burning marl that must have scorched his feet, making for comparatively open country on the tops of the hills, an unexpected move when the heat of the sun should have forced him to seek the cooler depths of the shady ravine. Fortunately the Banjaras were on that side with the gallant Subadar who, shouting : " Come on ! the tiger is escaping ! " together with the bold Naik charged at the head of the Banjaras and with wild yells drove the tiger grumbling down the hillside, pursued by a shower of sticks and stones. And now we could see Bhima in the distance, walking alone up the bed of the ravine, with beaters behind him and on either flank, and driving the tiger along with a flourish of his spear, as he said afterwards " as if it had been a sheep." The great beast entered the bamboo thicket in front of me, and I could hear him panting, for he was only twenty yards away. As the beat approached he burst from the thicket with a gruff roar, and charged across the open ground towards me, his eyes blazing, his ruff standing out like set bristles round his mighty head. My bullet caught him between the neck and shoulder, and he required no second shot ; he turned a complete somersault, lay gasping amid the rocks, and was dead in a few moments.

Thus ended a long chase entailing so many days of hard but pleasurable labour under a blazing sun ; but the end gained with so much labour is far more satisfactory than one easily attained. I already felt better, and as I climbed into the bullock-cart into which the tiger had already been hoisted at the entrance to the ravine, I was amply repaid for all I had gone through during the past week, and made a happy entry into camp. The tiger weighed over 500 pounds, as much as our scales could deal with, and we guessed it to be at least fifty pounds more.

The measurement between pegs placed at the nose and tip of the tail, taken in a straight line, came to 9 feet 8 inches, another peg at the root of the tail making the tail 3 feet. Measured round the curves of the body an addition of 6 or 8 inches might be made to the total length, but that is a very uncertain mode of measurement, and two people employing this method would probably arrive at different results. If the measurement were left to the shikari or other follower it would probably be a foot or so longer; he might make a few kinks in the tape, with the very natural though erroneous idea of adding to his master's glory. If all tigers were measured in a straight line between pegs there would be a possibility of accurate comparison, and we should never have heard of the 12-foot tigers so often recorded in old books and diaries. Many of these were measured from stripped skins, stretched to great lengths and adding from 2 feet upwards to the tiger's length. An old edition of a famous encyclopædia states that the tiger attains a length of 15 feet " to the tip of the tail " and that one has been recorded as 18 feet, the length of a very large python or boa constrictor. The tiger is an animal of fearful symmetry, and if a symmetrical tiger 12 feet in length be drawn on a wall, it will be realised that no such animal has existed in historical times; perhaps there was such a " monster of the prime " in the primeval days of such creatures as giant sloths and dinosaurs.

The Maharaja of Cooch Behar, an accurate observer, kept a careful record of 365 tigers shot in 37 years. The longest on his list -measured in a straight line from nose to tip 10 feet 5 inches, the tail being 3 feet 6 inches. Tails of northern India tigers are in general longer than those of the south, where they rarely exceed 3 feet and an inch or two. But the largest of the Maharaja's tigers had a body 7 feet 1½ inches long; the tail measured only 3 feet, but with the 3 foot 6 inch tail of the other one it would have been 10 feet 7½ inches in length, or 11 feet round the curves of the body. That may be taken as the extreme length of any tiger. It is interesting to note that the Maharaja weighed a tiger of 546 pounds and shot another he thought must have exceeded 600 pounds.

That night the shikaris held high revel. Two goats were given to them and slaughtered before the symbol of the Spirit of the Wild; rum was served out, and each one related his deeds of prowess, all having some strange tale to tell regarding the courage and the peculiar habits of the dead tiger. No doubt the great Ambari tiger and his destroyers will be long talked of in the surrounding country and in the villages from whence the beaters came to drive him from his lair, especially as each beater was given the double fee of eight annas, equivalent then to a shilling, in celebration of the event. Even so the hoof-beats of John Nicholson's charger were heard to resound in the Khyber Pass fifty years after his death at Delhi; and to this day Colonel Geoffrey Nightingale, who died on horseback in the act of spearing a panther on the Bolarum plain, is remembered in the Deccan jungles he long ranged in hunting tigers. In India it is men of action, warriors and hunters, who are remembered and have that immortality defined by Napoleon as " the memory we leave behind us in the minds of men."

The tigress still remained to be accounted for. Experience had proved that she did not lie up beside her kill, but was in the habit of leaving it at or before daybreak and retreating to a locality, probably in dense jungle, not yet discovered. We decided that the best way of bringing her to book would be to stalk and shoot her on the kill as soon as it was light enough to see. She had already killed three buffalo calves on the same spot. As I had the fortune to kill the Ambari tiger, and it was Robert's turn for a first chance, he started before daybreak and just at dawn arrived within a couple of hundred yards of the place where another calf had been picketed the day before. A bush-clad bank a few feet high overlooked the pool where the bait had been set. Robert, having taken off his boots, cautiously approached the bank, crept forward behind bushes, and peeped over, disturbing on the way a four-horned antelope which barked repeatedly as he approached. He saw the tigress lying not more than twenty yards off beside the carcass of her victim, and he at once opened fire, but being overexcited his first bullet only inflicted a slight wound, while the second passed through both haunches as she made off, and she subsided in the cover of low bushes and scattered trees and bamboos. The tigress then saw him and made a sudden rush, and he fired and knocked her over, while at the same time the bones of her hind legs appeared to give way. The brave beast now raised herself on her fore-paws, facing her assailants, wounded to death and unable to charge, a sight horrible to behold with blood pouring from her gaping jaws. Another shot put her out of her misery. This was a small tigress, under 8 feet in length and with a bright-coloured coat. But tigresses are generally a foot shorter than the male, and usually not much more than half the weight, although the Maharaja of Cooch Behar records one of 9 feet 5 inches, the length of an average male.

That evening we discussed the question of these

great beasts' method of hunting, whether by sight, hearing, or scent. We concluded that all three senses come into play, though in differing degrees, for it is improbable that any of these would remain unutilised. But I thought that they generally hunted by a combination of sight and hearing, all cats being quick to detect movement and sound, but possessing somewhat deficient powers of scent compared with the dog tribe. It is difficult to lay down the law where there is considerable difference of expert opinion, although most Indian sportsmen consider that the tiger and leopard do not use their sense of smell in hunting their prey. In some parts of the East, as in Annam, a dead bait rather than a living calf is generally used to attract the tiger, which is partial to high game. Usually in hunting tigers we pay no attention to the question of scent, and I instanced the case of the first tigress we killed in Shaikh Farid Kora, which drank at a pool where a buffalo broke loose and got away; that it drank before the calf got away was certain, for the tigress's tracks were in places obliterated by those of the calf. Then there was the calf left alive at the pool where the great tiger lay down during the thunderstorm on our first night in the Ganeshpur camp.

CHAPTER XIV

THE MONARCH OF THE GLEN

AFTER a day's rest for the shikaris and in order to dry the skins, a welcome respite from the strenuous hunts of the past days, we moved our camp farther to the east, a day's march from the valley of the river to which our operations had hitherto been confined, and pitched our tents under the great banyan tree at Singarwari, on the top of a pass over a range of low hills. This great tree had dropped many tendrils that had taken root in the ground and formed new trunks, some almost equal in size to the parent tree. This process, extending through many years, perhaps centuries, had resulted in an extensive grove composed of one tree whose offshoots formed arches and aisles of columned dropping stems over enough space to have afforded shade and cover to a body of horse a thousand strong. Indeed, old Nathu, who was acquainted with many traditions of the countryside, said that in 1818 Baji Rao, Peshwa of Poona, the leader of the Maratha Confederacy, had encamped here with his Maratha Horse when fleeing before the pursuing army of General Doveton.

Under this tree, or one of its columns, we sat on the afternoon of our arrival, while the shikaris and other followers and domesticated animals of every description were accommodated beneath the spacious leafy vault. Overhead were birds of many species.

There were green pigeons with their beautiful green, yellow, and mauve plumage, well described as " whistling as a schoolboy whistles under his breath," green paroquets, green flycatchers, and others of verdant hue, as well as mainas or starlings, doves, bulbuls, little owls, and noisiest of all, the koel and the coppersmith already described.

We had ridden some thirty miles from Ambari, and our tents were pitched near the brink of a small ravine beyond a broad valley enclosed by well-wooded hills. In the evening Robert and I strolled down to the edge of the ravine, when we saw a number of wild dogs run out on the far side, and as they stood at gaze after the manner of these animals, we shot one each, too late to save a hind sambar on whose remains they had been feasting in a glade below where they had done the poor animal to death. The weather was now very hot, and as we had a march of ten miles to our next camping-ground, we decided to start before daybreak in order to escape the heat of the sun. Everything was in readiness before we lay down to sleep, and at two o'clock in the morning we set out on the road through the forest, riding our ponies, the shikaris and others carrying our rifles and guns. The moon was shining brightly and we had gone some distance along a narrow path through dense jungle when there was a rustling noise as of some heavy animal among the dry leaves and a great bear rushed out at our party, uttering gruff roars. Robert was leading ; his pony reared up on its hindlegs and he slipped off and seized the rifle which Chandru was carrying at his side. But the bear was only making a hostile demonstration ; it turned tail and bolted back into the jungle when only a couple of yards off ; this was fortunate, for had it charged home someone might well have been severely damaged before a shot could be fired.

Soon after daybreak we met a noble-looking and courteous Banjara chieftain who told us that he had suffered great losses from the depredations of a tiger ; it had not only killed many cattle and one of his herdsmen, but also a valuable horse worth 500 rupees. He was now travelling with a herd of small bullocks, each carrying two blocks of salt on its back, driven by a dozen or more of his men. The tiger, he said, inhabited the broad valley already referred to, and he would be glad on his return to his camp, near which ours would be pitched, to give us all the help he could in hunting this destructive beast. At the camping ground we were met by the headman of the village, who told us that he had fled from English territory at the time of the Mutiny when all cattle were being commandeered for transport service with the troops. He was friendly and communicative regarding tigers in his neighbourhood, for news of our coming had preceded us, and our generous treatment of the famine-stricken people of the country through which we had passed was not without its effect.

Brook Sahib had now come up with his little flock of buffaloes, and by the time we had breakfasted our bullock-carts and camels had arrived. All set to at once and in an hour baggage was unloaded, tents were pitched, and everything looked as though the camp had been established a week or more in its present position. The tents stood under a group of trees in an open and cultivated plain of small extent, bounded on one side by hills overlooking the broad valley. They stood upon a plateau and in the misty distance we distinguished the blue hills of Ambari. Below the plateau on that side lay the broad valley, split up into numerous branches and filled with somewhat sparse jungle. The main watercourse was dry, but the deep ravines and clefts in the hills were well wooded and looked likely places for water and game.

On the other side of the camp, within a mile, a deep and wooded ravine took its rise in rocky ground. This nullah was at its head in the nature of a canyon, with rocky and precipitous sides, and its presence was not revealed until one came suddenly upon the brink. It intersected the forest as far as the eye could reach, eventually losing itself in the great river which drained the country on this side of the watershed we had crossed after leaving Ambari; we had passed from the valley of one great river into that of another. This ravine contained many pools of water and good cover for tigers. At its head a forest of dwarf teak trees extended to the outskirts of our camp.

I started after breakfast to explore this ravine, taking the Subadar and Nathu, together with a local shikari and a man with a couple of buffalo calves for picketing in case tracks were found. We followed the watercourse for some miles, but found nothing except tracks of bears and panthers, although the jungle looked excellent for tigers. However we picketed the calves at likely spots in case any tigers should visit so attractive a locality. Besides, the ground was very hard, the water that remained generally lay among rocks and tigers might be about in spite of the absence of tracks.

On my return to camp I found that Robert had been with Bhima, Chandru, and a couple of Banjaras to prospect the great valley. They had followed the main watercourse for the greater part of its length and found tracks, all some days old, of a large tiger and a tigress. Here also buffaloes were picketed, although the prospects did not look very promising, for the forest was too open and shadeless. It was already within half an hour of sunset when a herdsman came to tell us that a tiger had killed one of his cows close by and was still on the spot. It was too late to arrange a beat, especially as the tiger would be on the alert at this late hour. The place was only a few hundred yards off; what was to be done?

We soon made up our minds; we picked up our rifles, ran to our ponies, mounted them bare-backed, and rode off with the herdsman running ahead to guide us to the place. Arrived within a hundred yards, we dismounted and approached the kill.

"There it is!" said Robert, pointing to the dead cow, lying just as it had been killed.

"And there is the tiger!" I exclaimed, raising my rifle to fire. The beast was walking rapidly away among the tree trunks towards a dry channel leading down to the ravine, but it was not possible to get a shot between the intervening trees. We ran after it to the edge of the channel but it was already out of sight; we cut across the intervening ground to a point lower down, in the hope of intercepting it in a bend of the channel, but in vain. It was now getting dusk, and although we stayed within view of the kill as long as anything could be distinguished, the tiger did not return. Indeed, it never returned, for next morning we found the dead cow untouched. Such is the timidity and apparent fear of man of these great wild beasts that they will often leave their prey untouched when thus disturbed.

We separated into two parties after viewing the kill, Robert going to the great valley while I with the Subadar and some of the men went to view the buffaloes we had picketed in the ravine. We were disappointed to find that there had been no kill, and

I was returning disconsolately to camp when I met a big bear in the bed of the ravine at about twenty yards' distance. I shot him through the body, and he got up on his hind legs and embraced a tree, gnawing it with his teeth; I walked close up to him to try to induce him to charge, a foolish thing to do, for a wounded bear is not to be despised and I ought to have killed him at once. But he continued to claw and bite the tree, growling the while, and until another shot killed him. This was a very old bear with some of his teeth worn and broken, but he had a fairly good coat.

Meanwhile Robert with Bhima and Chandru had gone down into the great valley where he found that a buffalo had been killed by the big tiger; but the tiger had made off to a distance, for his departing tracks were visible a mile or two up the watercourse until they were lost on hard ground, and although the party traversed a large extent of jungle in the hope of finding the beast, they failed to discover his midday retreat. In the afternoon we amused ourselves trying to catch fish in a deep pool not far from camp. We got one murrell weighing about five pounds, an excellent fish for the table, although fastidious people might have been put off eating this one, for it had swallowed a good-sized snake that was taken out of its stomach by the cook.

During the next few days the big tiger killed two more buffaloes. We tried in vain to track him down to his unknown haunt, and beat for him twice, but the first time he was not at home, having already gone off to a distance. On the second occasion the shikaris went too near and disturbed him where he was lying in a pool of water at some distance from the kill; he went off across the valley, roaring angrily. It began to look as though there was to be a repetition of the events of Ganeshpur and **Ambari**. Day after day one or other of us rode to the head of the great valley, and descended on foot with the shikaris to the low ground where the beast's tracks were to be seen on many paths.

At length one day we came upon fresh tracks in a part not previously explored. We followed these for a mile or more, where we were able to pick them up at intervals by pools or in ground that took the impression of his great pads, splayed out to the size of a soup plate, showing him to be an old and mighty beast. The tracks led us into a precipitous and rocky ravine, filled with jungle and having no practicable egress except into the main valley. The ravine was so hidden that it might easily have been overlooked, but here were tracks of various dates; evidently we had traced the big tiger to his secluded retreat. We picketed a calf within this glen, and Bhima, while doing this, declared that he saw the tiger thirty yards off, but we could not get a view of it for a shot in those dense thickets. The animal had retreated towards the head of the ravine; it was already afternoon, we were seven miles from camp, and it was not possible to arrange a beat for that day; one more calf had to be added to the many sacrificed, but this tiger was worth it; he had killed a herdsman, though he had not eaten him, as well as many valuable cattle.

We started early next morning, taking forty beaters, for we were sure that there would be a kill. The beat was arranged with the greatest caution, the men being assembled on the plateau above the head of the ravine; stops were not to move forward to their posts until the guns had been placed at the opening into the main valley, where we took up positions to cover the whole exit from the glen. At length a shrill whistle gave the signal for the beaters to move forward. They crowded to the edge of the cliffs and clambered down the rocks, casting stones into the bushes and calling to the tiger to come out and be killed. Soon the great beast came out from a thicket into the open glade, holding his head fearlessly erect, his tongue lolling, his jaws slavering and dripping, for it was a day of burning heat. He stood at a distance of some fifty yards, his body shining golden in the noonday sun ; then he turned into a stony nullah leading direct to Robert's post and was lost to view.

There was an interval of a quarter of an hour ; the beaters continued to shout and climb slowly down the rocks ; I could not see Robert, but expected every moment to hear his shot. It was related afterwards that the tiger had lain down in some bushes with his head turned up-hill towards a tree occupied by a stop, and at length the man, seeing that the beaters were approaching and that the tiger would not move, clapped his hands and the great beast got up and turned across the nullah. And now I was surprised to see the tiger emerge from the jungle ten yards in front of me, seeming at that distance of primordial size, with vast expanse of chest, enormous head, and glowing eyes of fire, his great tongue hanging from his jaws, and the sound of his panting breath filling all the forest. He looked indeed the monarch of the glen.

I fired into his shoulder, and he spun round and round and appeared about to drop, but recovered and dashed forward uttering no sound, and disappeared in a patch of tall grass, followed by a second shot. I turned round, and as I looked saw him pitch forward on to his head, while his tail stood erect and he dropped out of sight. We now assembled and

THE TIGER SLAIN.

This noble animal had wandered over the valley for many years, and had now fallen to one ruthless bullet.

VULTURES.

These scavengers hunt by sight, and not by scent.

following to the place where I had last viewed him, found him lying dead in the grass. He was a splendid animal and had probably wandered over these valleys for many years, as the place was far from the haunts of man and had not been visited by other sportsmen. The ravine in which he now lay dead contained immense banyan and other trees, the growth of ages. The waters of many rainy seasons had poured down the declivity at the head of the glen, had hollowed out and filled a deep pool among the rocks, and had dripped to form gigantic stalactites which depended from the roof, the basin serving as a fine drinking place for tigers and other beasts frequenting this wide valley with its shady and sequestered ravines during countless ages. Amid these surroundings tracks proved that the tiger had long made his abode and found a quiet lair, issuing forth to prey on the deer and nilgai abounding in the forest, and taking his toll of cattle, though only one human life, when the herdsmen brought their flocks to these green pastures. And here at last this noble animal had fallen to one ruthless bullet.

We were up at daylight and visited the ravine where I shot the bear. The buffaloes picketed in the great valley were withdrawn, for the only other tracks worth considering were those of a tigress which appeared to have left the locality. We found a buffalo killed at the head of one of the branches of the ravine only three miles from camp and we were certain that the tiger responsible would be brought to bag, the sheer rocks on either side admitting of no escape, so that an animal lying up there was caught like a rat in a trap when the only egress was blocked by the fire of rifles.

The beaters were assembled and distributed in the usual manner, and before they began to advance, sundry roars announced that the game was afoot. Soon a tiger came trotting out towards Robert, who dropped it dead in its tracks with a bullet between the shoulders. Immediately afterwards there was a loud roar in the nullah, and a tigress came bounding along at great speed, taking exactly the same line as her companion. She sprang over the dead body of her predecessor, receiving Robert's bullet behind her shoulder, but galloped on in silence and fell dead in a bush, part of which she seized with her jaws and retained between her clenched teeth in her dying agony. On examining the dead calf we found that it had been clawed and bitten about the shoulders and elsewhere in many places; both the tigers were young and clumsy killers.

CHAPTER XV

SAFETY LAST!

IN the next beat, in itself presenting no unusual features, a long, lean tiger walked out in front of me. I was squatting behind a fallen tree, and did what should not have been done, firing a moment too soon when the tiger was coming straight towards me. The bullet made a grazing wound, striking the animal in the back and only making a long superficial cut in the skin and flesh and so failing to penetrate. The tiger dashed on, being missed with my second barrel. Then a panther walked out along the watercourse fifteen yards or so from me just ahead of the beaters, and I shot it dead. The beaters were at once warned to stop and climb trees as there was a wounded tiger afoot. But the irrepressible Nathu was not far off, walking in front of the men; he saw the panther struggling in the throes of death, and at once ran forward and began to belabour it with his staff, although I told him not to be a fool in running such risks, for the beast might recover sufficiently to attack him. But Nathu had no respect for panthers, considering that the tiger was the only animal not to be despised. Fortunately the panther was at its last gasp, and expired while the blows were being showered upon its body.

In the valley ahead of me was a shallow watercourse running through a wide grass patch, several acres in extent, whilst on either side the jungle was burnt and bare. The wounded tiger's tracks led up this channel, and, walking abreast, Robert and I with the Subadar, the shikaris following with spare guns, followed slowly for a hundred yards or so. But it was a winding course and there was so much danger in the long grass that we might come upon the tiger suddenly at very close quarters, and have it on to us before there was time to stop the charge, that we left the grass patch and went out to one side to consult as to further operations. Looking ahead, I saw that the watercourse, now quite dry from the heat of summer, took a bend outwards and left the grass, winding into the bare burnt ground for some distance. This bend was about 300 yards ahead. Robert and I and the Subadar decided to make for this point, and see whether the tiger's tracks passed it, with a view to locating the position of the beast as far as possible. I was so placed when we went forward that I had the first view of the bed of the channel, and as I looked I saw the wounded beast, its back smeared with blood, lying down under a small tree within six feet of me; the tiger raised his head, his green eyes glowed, and then I shot him through the heart, Robert firing a moment afterwards to make sure that the beast should not be able to get up. All was over in a second. The tiger did not hear our approach, owing to the soft surface of burnt grass under foot, or we would perhaps have fared badly, for he was only slightly wounded in the first instance, and even at the point of death the charge might well have reached us.

This incident may be taken to show that the principle of "safety first" should have no place in hunting dangerous wild beasts. It may be said that "safety last" is a better watchword, particu-

SAFETY LAST!

larly in following up a wounded animal, the chief danger in big game hunting. This does not mean that one's safety should not be considered, but that it ought to be put in its proper place. The first consideration is the killing of the game by a well-placed shot so as to cause as little suffering as possible and to reduce the probability of its reaching cover. This requires an effective weapon, a cool head, and a steady hand. But instances arise, either as in this case from the hastiness or excitement of youth or inexperience, or other cause, of an animal getting away to cover, when it must be followed, both to release it from further suffering and to secure the quarry.

But there is another and still more urgent reason. A wounded tiger or other dangerous beast is prone to attack and kill any human being who comes near it, while in some instances the beginning of a career of man-eating has been traced to wounds causing the animal to become hostile to human beings owing to the suffering inflicted by man; or else to its being incapacitated from hunting or killing deer or cattle and so turning on man as an easier prey. Safety to the hunter must therefore be a secondary consideration. Tigers are found and hunted not only in more or less secluded and unfrequented spots, but in the neighbourhood of villages whose inhabitants go into the jungle to graze their cattle or to gather wood and the fruits of the forest. To these a wounded beast or a man-killer is a terrible danger. Tigers and panthers have been shot close to roads by which people pass by; on one occasion I had to hold up traffic in both directions while dealing with a wounded panther in roadside bush cover. The hunter, while taking due precautions consistent with his object, should put " safety " in its proper place.

Next morning a woodcutter came with information that he had seen two small tiger cubs the evening before lying in a hole among some rocks five miles off, but he was afraid to take them as the tigress roared at him when he approached the spot. We walked to the place, led by the woodcutter; the tigress had already carried off her young in her mouth, as a cat carries her kittens, and the only evidence of their presence on the ground, where no tracks were visible, was in the scattered hairs in the hole where they were lying. We searched all likely cover in the neighbourhood, but could find no further trace of mother and cubs. On the way back a cobra six feet long was seen making off in front of us; I seized a spear from Chandru and ran it through the body, whereupon the reptile reared up with expanded hood, pinned and helpless, but presenting a very evil aspect; it was soon battered to death with stones.

Meanwhile there was plenty to do in camp, skins requiring a great deal of attention while they were lying pegged out in the shade during this hot weather. We were greatly interested in their preservation, and did not leave all the work to our men, although they were quite competent to do it. But we considered that a naturalist and sportsman, and the two are properly inseparable, or at least every hunter should be a naturalist, should be able to do these things with his own hands, or indeed how could he know that they were properly done?

We saw this day near a pool of water an ambush constructed by a village shikari who had hung on a branch of his lair the skin of a monkey filled with sand, intended to bring him luck like the fetishes used by African and West Indian believers in the virtues of Obi. From this ambush the shikari was in the habit of shooting animals that came down to drink, killing deer, antelope, and other creatures regardless of age or sex, or season. The man had only a matchlock, a very primitive weapon, so he could seldom get any game by the methods which we regard as legitimate. No doubt such poachers do a great deal of damage, but it has to be remembered that they are very poor and largely dependent for food on the animals they shoot or trap.

Some primitive aboriginal and wandering tribes live mainly by this means; they have lived for ages on the produce of the forest and the chase, and it is hard on them to take away their means of livelihood. The pardis, whose encampment we had seen during one of our marches, are very skilful in noosing antelope. When a herd is seen in a field or other suitable locality, they set a number of nooses along an extended front, sometimes using a stalking bullock under cover of which they approach without alarming the herd. The antelope are then driven over the nooses, and a number are caught by this contrivance. Sometimes they break one or more legs of the unfortunate creatures in order to take them without trouble to market and dispose of them as fresh meat. They also catch quantities of hares, partridges, quail, and other small game in nets or nooses. Many cruelties used to be practised in disabling captive animals, often kept for days with legs or wings broken to prevent their escape, the eyelids of birds being fastened together with pieces of split cane.

In Mysore and other parts of India even tigers are netted. Nets are spread over wells inhabited by pigeons and the occupants are thus captured, the eggs or young, if the latter are old enough, being taken from the nests. Quail are assembled by means of call-birds placed out in the fields in small wicker cages, and then netted in great numbers. The wildfowl exposed for sale in Calcutta market are generally netted, but in some parts the natives have a very ingenious method of catching wild duck. A number of round earthenware pots are floated out from the shore of a lake into the middle of a pack of duck; at length the birds become accustomed to these unusual objects and pay no attention to them. Then the shikari swims out with his head in a large pot having eyeholes in it; arriving in the midst of the unsuspecting birds, he skilfully draws them under water one after another by the legs, tucking their necks under the waistband that forms his only article of clothing.

In the Punjab grey cranes in winter flock southwards in large numbers from their summer haunts in high Asia and are captured when migrating; they fly very low at night, uttering their peculiar cry; they are caught by means of slings or bolas made of stones attached to long pieces of cord, flung into the midst of a passing flock. Perhaps the most extraordinary method of hunting is that known in Southern India as " shikar with bells," which may by now have been forgotten and disused. Two men take part in the hunt on dark and moonless nights. One man bears on his head a receptacle containing lighted oil wicks and in his hand a chime of bells. The man with lights and bells dances ahead of his companion with grotesque antics, and the fire and tintinnabulation of the bells appear to attract and fascinate animals. The animal stands rooted to the spot or is irresistably drawn towards the shikaris and shot down at close range. In this manner even tigers are said to be killed. Similarly in our own country salmon have been speared by torchlight.

We had now moved camp ten miles farther to the

east, but news of tigers was disappointing. The medicine-chest came into requisition, for in the village near our camping-ground the population generally, and the children in particular, were suffering from sores on the legs, probably due to bad water and scanty food. We were able to give some relief as well as to prescribe and supply such necessary drugs as quinine for fever and other ailments. The effects of famine were apparent in this part of the country although it was not densely populated. Cattle were dying in great numbers and their bones strewed the countryside, their loss adding to the general distress, while the tanners were doing a good trade in collecting the hides.

On the second night of our stay at this camping-ground, a donkey was killed close to the village a couple of miles off. We walked over to the place next morning and found the carcass partly eaten. The ground was hard, so no tracks were to be seen, but the small fang-holes in the throat, the fact that the dead animal was not dragged away or carried off, and was eaten only at the chest between the fore-legs, and the locality of the kill, so near the village, indicated the work of a panther; several were known to be in the neighbourhood. It was decided that Robert should sit up over the kill. The night would now be pitch dark, and anything would be invisible unless seen against the skyline. So a hole was dug in the ground close by and covered over with a native charpoy or wood and string bedstead, heaped with branches after Robert had got into the hole at dusk. The men who accompanied him to fix up the ambush waited in the village.

Scarcely had the men gone when, like a ghost from the gloom of night, a great panther appeared within a few feet of the watcher, its head and massive neck clearly outlined against the star-lit sky. A shot was followed by a roar, a sound of struggling on the ground, a few deep-drawn groans, and then all was still. Five minutes elapsed, and, as Robert related afterwards, he was thinking of whistling up the men, when another panther was outlined against the sky, and met with a similar fate. Should he now call the men, for there was a doubt whether the last animal was dead, or even hit?

He cogitated for a quarter of an hour; the position was cramped and uncomfortable; he raised the whistle to his lips and was about to blow a blast when at that moment the carcass moved. He grasped his rifle and peered into the deepening gloom, perhaps making a slight noise, for the panther at the kill raised its head and gazed intently, with ears cocked. A flash of flame from the ambush, and the beast fell with a deep groan and died straightway. After waiting five minutes and hearing no sound, he whistled up the men, who released him from his uncomfortable ambush. Then by the light of a lantern they found three dead panthers, an old female and two cubs, male and female, nearly as big as herself. The old one had seized the donkey so firmly in her jaws that they had closed tightly and a great piece of flesh had to be cut off with a knife as the jaws could not be forced asunder. On the way back to camp, Robert came upon an extraordinary animal on the path, a scaly ant-eater or pangolin about three feet long; one of the men hit it with his stick, whereupon it rolled itself up into a ball presenting a hard horny surface, protected by armour plating against its enemies.

We had now arrived on the verge of a great forest some thirty miles wide, unknown to all in our camp. To enter and march through would be to plunge into an unexplored wilderness, but an examination of the map made fifty years before showed a more favourable-looking country beyond the forest belt, containing mountains, rivers, lakes, and some scattered villages; it should hold abundance of game. But before marching on into this forest we picketed out buffaloes in a cover a few miles off, where we found tracks of a tigress; she made demonstrations when the men went to look next day whether there had been a kill, charging out when they ventured near, and roaring at them angrily.

She killed two buffaloes, and we arranged the beat through a rather densely wooded ravine. But the beaters from the village were not used to the work, and showed not unnatural timidity, making off as soon as the game was afoot, so the tigress broke back without showing herself. The same thing occurred in another beat; she charged out at the line and the men fled precipitately in all directions, but this time Robert and the Subadar accompanied the beat and when the tigress made for a group of beaters, and would probably have got home and mauled some of them if she had not been stopped, they shot her dead in full career. She was a gallant beast, and perhaps had cubs hidden somewhere in the jungle, but none could be found in that dense cover.

Generally the villagers in these wilds are courageous enough in driving out dangerous game. Most men would feel some trepidation in starting, armed with nothing more formidable than a stick or an axe, to drive out a tiger; yet there is seldom any difficulty in obtaining beaters who do their duty for a poor pittance of a few pence. But it is a principle never to send in men when there is a wounded and dangerous animal afoot. If a tiger is wounded, let the sportsman follow it up by himself, or take only men provided with firearms and competent to use them.

We were now about to enter the country of the aboriginal Gonds, one of those jungle tribes of whom at the time there were some 50,000 in this State. It may be doubted whether the Gond population is any greater than it was in those days, and it has very probably decreased, partly through causes pointed out by Captain James Forsyth in his *Highlands of Central India*, where he refers to the improvidence and the hardships these children of the forest have to contend with. They were then addicted to most intemperate habits, and with them, as he says, " occasional periods of hardship are sure to be followed by outbursts of excess; and thus the life of the Gond has usually intervals of severe toil succeeded by periods of unrestrained dissipation, in which anything he may have earned has been squandered in drink." Improved administration may have bettered their condition, but in most countries contact with Western and other " civilising " influences appears generally to result in the destruction of those races commonly termed inferior. Whether they and their social systems are really inferior to those of Europe is perhaps open to philosophic doubt. It has been said that it is a pity America was " discovered," with the resulting degeneration of indigenous races and the disappearance of the buffalo and other fauna, a philosophic truth stated by the infant William Hazlitt, who wrote at eight years of age: " I think it would have been a great deal better if the white people had not found it (America) out. Let the others have it to themselves for it was made for them."

CHAPTER XVI

ABORIGINAL GONDS

IN all countries aboriginal tribes, where they are not exterminated as is so often the case, are driven by invading hordes into remote and comparatively inaccessible regions where they hope to find safety from molestation or at least from intrusion, and where they naturally in course of time adapt themselves to the mode of life best suited to their environment. And who shall say that such savages do not live a happier life than the peoples who are bound to the wheel of our own form of civilisation! Indeed, it is surely a crime to disturb the pathetic contentment of such peoples and to teach them our ways and inflict on them political and social habits and customs that have been so great a source of misery to the peoples of Europe.

India is no exception to this rule of the self-imposed isolation of aboriginal tribes. In the mountainous and forest-clad country about the great rivers —the Narbada, the Tapti, the Godavery, and the Krishna—, the aboriginal Gonds as well as other and allied and distinct tribes are found occupying many wild jungle tracts where they share with savage beasts the fastnesses of forest and mountain. These people are simple and primitive in mental and physical characteristics, in religion, and in habits. Their skins are very black. They have no written language, and no history but that of tradition handed down in the tribal community. Their age-old religion is animist, based on terror of the forces of Nature, of wild animals and other natural objects, trees, mountains, and rocks, common to the regions they inhabit, although where they have come into contact with more civilising influences they have to some extent been infected with Hinduism. For the Hindu pantheon has a tendency like Aaron's rod to swallow up lesser and more primitive deities, although it may take some of them to its bosom.

The aborigines vary in different parts of the country. Some are of comparatively fine physique, although their growth is usually stunted, probably by the hardness of their lives and the inferiority of their food. At any rate they have the advantage that they must by nature live dangerously, although that advantage, at one time the free choice of civilised man, has been increasingly made universal by the "blessings of civilisation" in the form of machinery and of modern war.

In remoter regions the aboriginals wear little clothing, often no more than a scanty rag, while some, like the dwarfed Chenchus of the Nallamallai Hills, have a rag hanging down behind as their sole garment, for all the world like the tail of a monkey, an animal to which they bear some resemblance. They live largely on the produce of the chase and the products of the forests they inhabit, collecting in due season wild mangoes, the fruit of the bher (*zizyphus jujuba*), ebony, and other trees, and the fleshy blossoms of the mohwa tree already described, eating its dry petals and distilling *daru*, an intoxicating liquor that furnishes a prominent feature of their feasts and orgies. But they also cultivate coarse millet and other grains and pulse in the fields round their villages or in clearings in the jungle. Sometimes they are sporadically nomadic, but they are often settled in large communities under their Rajas, who are often of fair complexion and sometimes of high caste Hindu origin.

In the Deccan they cultivate plots of land for a few years, and when the soil is exhausted rebuild their habitations of wattle, daub, and logs in a fresh locality. They make clearings in the forest for the cultivation of their crops, fertilising the ground with the ashes of burnt stumps of trees felled for building. Often they cultivate an area for not more than three years, partly perhaps because the soil, without a rotation of crops, is unproductive for a longer period ; but no doubt at times they abandon such clearings and migrate, often to evade the land tax when this is in some districts remitted for the first three years of occupation of fresh territory. They suffer severely in times of famine, or did in days gone by before the country was opened up by rail and road, and before famine relief was organised systematically by a benevolent government.

I have observed that in years of drought Nature has provided a more abundant crop of many forest products, and in such seasons of scarcity there often appears to be a more plenteous yield of mohwa and other fruits, and sometimes a general seeding of the bamboos, said to occur only once in thirty years, when a plentiful supply of seeds is afforded for human food as a substitute for rice to which it bears much resemblance. Such a general seeding occurred during the expedition which I am now describing. In times of drought also wild animals suffer from want of water, and deer and antelope are more easily killed both by beasts of prey and by the Gond hunters, for water is restricted in both quantity and distribution, and where water is, there the wild animals congregate.

The gods of the Gonds are dwellers of forest and mountain, the Great Spirit of the pantheist in its varied manifestations, not far removed from the deities of many other religions. For is not the Spirit everywhere and all-pervading, and what is that but pantheism, the presence of the divine essence in every living thing? As a Frenchman remarked to me long ago on a ship in the Black Sea: "*Les Anglais sont comme le bon Dieu, ils sont partout.*" So the god of the animist Gonds inhabits all nature and may be materialised in the tiger, the incarnation of terror, or the bison, the embodiment of physical strength, or in a mountain, a valley, a spring, a tree, and indicated or symbolised by, but not immanent in the red-painted stone so often met with in this narrative. The great god Pan may be half a beast or wholly an animal, such as the Great White Tiger, called forth to aid the Gonds against man-eaters or other destructive beasts, and whose tracks, larger than those of any tiger, may be seen on the paths round the villages on the morning after his help has been invoked with ceremonies very like those of Abraham of old, including the sacrifice of a goat or a fowl.

Their religious practices are mainly concerned with the propitiation of evil spirits, the manifestations of the wrathful god, whether these be the malignant ghosts of the victims of man-eaters or the destructive powers of epidemic diseases such as cholera and smallpox. The spirits of the victims of wild beasts are regarded as malignant, presumably taking on the attributes of their destroyers whom they warn of the approach of danger. The rajas who rule these communities are reputed to have the power of protecting the tiger from the bullets of the hunter's rifle, and they have to be propitiated.

South of the Tapti River in the Satpura Hills are the Korkus, a race kindred to the Gonds, but apparently more closely related to the Kols and Santals of the head waters of the Narbada. They are a mild and harmless people, but they suffered much from invading hordes of Moslems and Marathas in bygone days. Armies marched through their country from northern India to the south, and marauding Pindari robbers invaded their fastnesses, traversing the passes of the Satpuras. Where the wild tribes once dwelt in the more fertile valleys, they have been dispossessed by Hindus and driven to more secluded haunts among the eternal hills. In the mountains south of the Tapti is the River of Blood, the scene of the massacre of a whole aboriginal tribe by a band of Arabs in the service of a Maratha Chief.

But there were offerings and immolations more terrible than those of the simple forest-dwelling Gonds. On the island of Mandhata in the Narbada River is a sacred precipitous cliff from the summit of which devotees used to hurl themselves to destruction at the shrine of Shiva, the Hindu god, the Destroyer, also symbolised as Kali of tigerish propensities:

> Dark goddess of the azure flood,
> Whose robes are wet with infant tears,
> Skull-chaplet wearer, whom the blood
> Of men delights three thousand years. . . .

Kali, the goddess of death and destruction, whose weapon is a thunderbolt, whose steed is a bull, whose necklace is fashioned with human skulls, and on whose clotted hair is borne the Ganges flood. Fit emblem of Death! On the banks of the sacred river the thin acrid spires of smoke ascend from the funeral pyres of a thousand burning corpses, while foul vultures perch upon the bodies of the myriad dead, borne eastwards upon the broad bosom of Mother Ganges.

At Omkar on Mandhata in 1822 an Englishman witnessed the sacrifice of the last victim of that fearful rite, except for a poor old woman who shrank back at the last moment and was pushed over the brink by the excited pilgrims who had come to witness the tragedy. In the instance of 1822 the witness tried to dissuade the victim, a young man, from his fell purpose, offering him protection and a competence for life. But in vain. The devotee climbed to the summit and stood upon a rock, and " stepping back was lost to view for a moment—a pause that caused the head to swim, the heart to sink, the flesh to creep. The next second he burst upon our agonised sight in a most manful leap, descending feet foremost with terrific rapidity till, in mid career, a projecting rock reversed his position and caused a headlong fall. Instant death followed this descent of ninety feet, and terminated the existence of this youth whose strength of faith and fortitude would have adorned the noblest cause, and must command admiration when feelings of horror have subsided." This fearful rite, like that of sathi, the self-immolation of widows on the funeral pyres of their husbands, has been suppressed by a beneficent English Government.

These hills of the Narbada and the Tapti comprise a splendid country, one of the unspoilt regions of the earth, remote from the devastating track of the railway. Mountain is piled on mountain, not only grassy and forest-clad slopes, rising to giant peaks nearly 5000 feet above the level of the sea, but scarred cliffs of basalt or red sandstone descend sheer to valleys whose depths are hidden by forest trees where rushing torrents pour through silent glades. The greatest Indian wild oxen inhabit these vast solitudes, the old bulls separating from the herd to lead a lonely life or sometimes to wander in company with younger bulls who may have been driven from the cows by the stronger of their fellows. These solitary animals are reputed to be very fierce, but are generally timid and mild-tempered. The old hunters of long ago, armed with inferior and short-ranging weapons, necessitating a very near approach to the game, invested with a false character for ferocity many of the wild beasts they encountered. The bison is the chief god of the Korkus, who, however, do not object to their being hunted, although they do not like to touch the dead animal. The ferocity of this splendid beast with massive spreading horns, chestnut-coloured coat turning black in old bulls, and white stockings, has certainly been exaggerated, as has that of the buffalo, although both these oxen are fierce-looking animals and can be formidable when wounded. Probably few sportsmen would care to destroy many of these noble beasts.

The man-eater is supposed by the Gond to be accompanied by the spirit of its last victim, who gives warning of the presence or approach of an enemy of that victim's destroyer. The story of a man-eating tiger over the corpse of whose victim a native hunter took post in a tree, when the spirit warned the monster of danger, has often been related: The corpse raised a hand and pointed to the lurking shikari, whereupon the man-eater retreated. The hunter got down, pegged down the offending hand with a bamboo slip, and resumed his vigil in another tree ; the other hand repeated the warning on the next approach, with the same result ; but, having picketed that hand also, the hunter again went into ambush, and the tiger was shot when it came again, for there was no free hand to indicate his presence.

Our first march into the great forest brought us to a small Gond hamlet where water was so scarce that we had great difficulty in supplying our camp from the only muddy pool. The people here had never seen a white man, and were at first timid and difficult to approach. But we soon found that they were amenable to kind and generous treatment, especially when we had enlisted the services of an old hunter, Indru, who had great influence with his fellow-tribesmen, and who accompanied us for the next fortnight. He must have been seventy years old, for he had seen two seedings of the bamboos, and the third was now in progress. The Gonds ascribed to him a miraculous power over wild beasts, although this did not save him from being mauled by a bison in his youth, nor in the end from being killed by one of these animals.

Indru had hunted these jungles for many years and had slain many wild beasts with his rusty matchlock. The bison that wounded him had ripped up his thigh, and two years after the time of which I write he was killed by a bull he had wounded ; perhaps he had lost agility in his old age, for he was rushed and trampled under foot in a moment, as shown by the tracks and other indications seen by those who found the dead hunter. There in the forest where he fell his ashes were buried, and there as he would wish,

> "Indru, that great Hunter—the Wild Ox
> Stamps o'er his Head, but cannot break his Sleep."

We emerged next day from the great forest and came out into an open country near the shore of a large lake, surrounded by pastures where herds of cattle were grazing, while below the ancient anicut or embankment that penned in the water were acres of emerald green rice fields. Flocks of waterfowl dotted the lake, although the migratory species had long since winged their way to summer haunts where they nested in distant countries beyond the Himalayas. But there were a few comb-ducks, some ruddy sheldrakes, packs of reddish feathered whistling teal, and cotton teal, the latter like diminutive geese with bronze and white plumage, flying to and fro across the lake. The rough backs of crocodiles appeared above the surface, and some of these reptiles were sunning themselves on the bank. On the far shore of the lake, more than a mile distant, was an old mud and stone fort, nestling amid palms and other trees, containing the dwelling house of the Gond Raja.

The Subadar with a couple of mounted men at once went to convey our greetings to the Raja, and at three o'clock in the afternoon a discordant noise of tom-toms and drums announced the approach of the Chief of the Gonds to pay us a ceremonial visit. Soon the procession appeared in the distance and we went as far as the outskirts of the camp to receive the Raja on his State visit. He was riding in a small wagon covered with a red cloth and drawn by a pair of white bullocks, and was followed by a dozen or more retainers carrying spears, axes, matchlocks, and other primitive weapons. We advanced to meet him, shook hands as soon as he alighted from his carriage, and conducted him to a chair placed on a carpet outside the tents, where we all sat together, his and our retainers standing round us, except for the Raja's Minister and the Subadar, who also had chairs.

The Raja was a gentleman in appearance, manner, and speech, of fair complexion, deeply pock-marked, having only one eye, the other no doubt destroyed by the disease that had scarred his face. His Minister, curiously enough, was a Moslem of venerable appearance, with a long beard which he stroked with his right hand as he remarked after every sentence, however trivial, that issued from his Master's lips: " Bravo, what wisdom ! " The Raja promised to give us all possible assistance in hunting tigers, saying that there were several in the neighbourhood ; he brought gifts of a goat and some fowls, and in half an hour left, well-pleased with his visit and the ceremony with which he had been received. He had never before spoken with a white man.

It is customary in the East to return State visits within an hour or so, and five o'clock on the same afternoon saw us on our way to call on the Raja. We formed an imposing cavalcade, Robert and I riding in front, followed by the Subadar at the head of the remaining mounted men, and after them the shikaris and other camp followers of similar standing. They carried rifles, guns, spears, and all the weapons that we had ; the camel brought up the rear, laden with a tent and a saddle for presentation to the Raja.

He received us at the gateway of the fort and conducted us to an open verandah in front of his dwelling-house where preparations for our reception had been made with country-woven carpets and the only three chairs besides his own that he possessed, for he was very poor although he maintained a proper and dignified ceremonial. His Minister stood behind the Raja's chair during the durbar, the remainder of both parties, as well as the Raja's young son, were grouped as at our own reception at the camp.

The Raja told us that the fort was a thousand years old, having been the stronghold of his predecessors for many centuries; they formerly ruled all the surrounding country, but now his domain was very much reduced. The fort was a battered ruin with palms and other trees growing out of the crumbling mud walls and battlements. The population of the village, formerly a prosperous town of two thousand inhabitants, had dwindled to two hundred souls. There were three lakes, artificially formed by damming streams or watercourses; the largest, a mile in width and of about the same length, having a very wide solid dam or anicut, constructed by the Raja's ancestors and, as in the case of many public works, whether dams, bridges, or forts, a pious member of the family had been built up alive in the embankment to propitiate the spirit of destruction who might otherwise bring it to ruin. Such traditions are no doubt founded on fact, human skeletons having been disinterred from the ruined walls of fortresses and other buildings.

The Raja had only once before seen a European, when he had paid a visit to the great native city three hundred miles away; and he had never spoken to one and was in consequence somewhat nervous at first. But his courteous and dignified bearing made a great impression on us and confirmed him in our esteem, while his pleasure in accepting our poor presents was very gratifying, and our regard was increased by his friendliness and proffers of assistance in every way during our stay in his domain. I saw him again in after years, and found that the tent we gave him was always used for State ceremonies;

I was sorry to hear of his death soon after my last visit. Such kindly and pleasant men, together with many faithful friends and followers in the country we have left forever, with whom we have passed so many well-remembered years but who have now gone like ships that pass in the night, add to the store of memories which go to make India indeed a Land of Regrets to all who have given to it the best years of their lives.

Next day we moved our camp round the lake to a beautiful site on the farther shore not far from the Raja's fort, where great trees sheltered us from the noonday sun, now in May at its hottest in a brazen sky. Close by were some Hindu temples built of massive granite, some in a ruinous state, "two or three columns and many a stone," no longer used for religious ceremonies. In the thicket close by we found the remains of a calf killed by a panther, perhaps the same beast that a few days before had carried off and devoured a boy from a village a couple of miles off.

Early next morning, there having been no kill, Robert went out to prospect for tigers, while the Subadar and I skirted the shores of the lake with our guns to shoot some wild fowl for the pot. We stalked a large pack of cotton teal that lay close to the bank, where a clump of toddy palms covered our approach. When the teal rose, we brought down half a dozen birds, and Nathu, despite the crocodiles, plunged into the water waist-deep and soon recovered them. The report of the guns put up all the birds within a quarter of a mile, and we waited under the palms until a flock of red-brown whistling teal came flying slowly overhead, uttering their shrill cries. Our four barrels added five of these birds to the bag, and we returned to camp before Robert arrived from

ABORIGINAL GONDS

prospecting within a mile or two of our tents. He and the shikaris reported that there were at least half a dozen tigers in the neighbourhood, and they had arranged to picket buffalo calves in likely spots where a nullah with many tracks crossed the road. In the afternoon we went to fish in one of the smaller lakes on the other side of the fort, and in a couple of hours caught three or four dozen of small piran and dhok, which furnished a pleasant change from the usual diet of goat's flesh and fowls and eggs.

We thought how delightful it would be to settle down in this beautiful spot 150 miles from the nearest railway and with plenty of large and small game close by. We could build a house on the embankment, have a boat on the lake, and shoot and fish all day long. But it would be unpleasant and unhealthy in the rainy season and there would be great difficulties to overcome in the way of supplies and servants. So on the whole we came to the conclusion that it would be better to live elsewhere and visit the jungles in the Raja's domain for a month or two whenever possible. This conclusion was confirmed when a terrific thunderstorm came on in the evening; our tents were flooded in a moment and we had to take shelter in the deserted temples, where there was plenty of room for the whole camp.

Certainly the surroundings were most attractive in fine weather, and my thoughts after all these years often return with regretful longing to those far-off days and distant scenes. And then I turn to the views of Henry Bates in his *Naturalist on the Amazons*, who says that, after three years of England when he had been thirteen years in tropical America, he found " how incomparably superior is civilised life where feelings, tastes, and intellect find abundant nourishment, to the spiritual sterility of a half-savage existence, even though it be passed in the garden of Eden." Everyone to his taste! But Bates lived in the nineteenth and not in the twentieth century.

CHAPTER XVII

THE EMPIRE OF NIGHT

IN the preceding pages the fascination of night in the forest has often been described or referred to and much has been said of the sights to be seen by moonlight and the sounds that live in darkness, when so many creatures wander abroad. Then, indeed, "Night, that was before creation, watches sphinx-like, starred with eyes." One night there was a kill in the nullah that crossed the road, a wide, deep watercourse or ravine containing only an occasional pool and little shade. Before the beat began I observed a tigress emerge from tall grass on the farther bank and spring down into the channel, coming in my direction. Presently she left the watercourse and came along the bank, turning her flank towards me and stopping behind some bushes not very far off; I could hear her panting. I fired two shots, and being impatient, hit her through the hind leg, my bullets being deflected by bushes. She galloped out into the open, and Robert, who was quite fifty yards off, dropped her dead with a fine shot, turning her over like a rabbit in a ride.

Next day another kill was reported in a valley on the far side of the lake. A tigress was coming along straight towards Robert when a foolish stop, who did not know his business, began to hammer on a tree; with a muttered growl the tigress sprang forward, dashing through the jungle at great speed, and Robert missed her with both barrels, which was not surprising for he saw her only for a moment as she sped between the tree trunks. The shikaris at once concluded that this animal was under the special protection of the sylvan deity, for, said they, in all our wanderings how many tigers have we seen and slain? The sahibs' bullets never miss, and of the tigers seen not one has escaped with its life. Surely there is magic here!

The events that followed only served to confirm these simple-minded people in their belief. That night the tigress killed another buffalo picketed at the same spot, under a clump of trees near a pool of clear water among rocks. This time the animal went off before the beat began without giving anyone a glimpse of her striped coat.

"Now what are we to do?" I asked in despair.

"Sahib, this is not tiger, it is a *shaitan* (devil)!" said Bhima.

"*Shaitan* or not, we must have another try!" I exclaimed.

Then we agreed to leave the partly-eaten calf, covering up the remains to preserve them from vultures that were already hovering in the sky above, and to stalk the tigress at or just before daylight. We were on the spot before the first flush of dawn, but the tigress had just left for some unknown haunt, leaving the reeking carcass on which she had been feeding during the night.

She had now become so cunning or timid that there was no likelihood of our bringing her to bag by daylight, so we decided to sit up over the kill, and machans or platforms were prepared accordingly in the clump of trees. These were built of strong wood and surrounded by screens made of branches and leaves with an aperture to shoot through.

The branches with leaves were not placed until the afternoon, for when the leaves dried they would rustle with every movement of the occupant. A blanket and a pillow were placed in each machan, for it is not possible to sit still if one is in a state of discomfort, and any creaking or rustling would scare away a tiger.

It is related that an inexperienced sportsman was fond of luxury; his servant brought his dinner and handed it up to him where he was watching in a machan over a kill, not forgetting the champagne. But it was curious that, notwithstanding the popping of the cork, the tiger came and was shot very soon after the servant had departed. In reality this is what might be expected, for the sportsman probably had an interval of quiescence while the tiger, seeing and hearing the men depart, thought that the coast was clear and that it was safe to return to his feast.

Late in the afternoon we settled down in our ambushes. It had been arranged that Robert was to have the first shot, and no animal was to be fired at until the tiger came. There would be moonlight during the early part of the night, but we were to remain at our posts until morning. We could see not only the ravine and the kill but could look right across the lake and hear the distant lowing of cattle being driven home at sunset. As the sun set, dark forms could be distinguished in the neighbouring glades, and soon a herd of spotted deer approached the water, among them a fine stag. They came along cautiously, stopping now and then to listen and look round or browse on the low-hanging branches of trees. They passed quite close, and then I made a slight movement; a hind looked up, gave the warning note of alarm, and in a moment all disappeared in the deepening shades of the forest. Then a train of langur monkeys came through the branches of overhanging trees, and it was ludicrous to watch their fear and caution when they approached the pool. A monkey would come down and almost reach the water's edge, and then dash up a tree with an expression of terror, showing his white teeth, although there was nothing in sight to alarm him. A large grey mongoose with russet face and feet and a black tip to his tail trotted up the bank; grey junglefowl, little spurfowl, and painted quail came pattering over the dry leaves, where even the stirring of a lizard was plainly heard.

It was getting dark, and still no tiger came. We looked out across the lake where all was silent except for the cry of a night-bird, and the shadows of the forest advanced across the water. The half-moon now shone on the scene, the silent pool, the remains of the kill, the deserted bush and water-course, while an unpleasant smell rose from the carcass. Still nothing came; the moon dropped lower and lower; I heard the tread of a heavy animal, and grasped my rifle, peering into the deepening gloom; a striped form slunk from shadow to shadow and approached the kill, but as the shape of the animal was more distinctly outlined, it was seen to be a hyena; I threw a cartridge at it, Robert moved in his machan, and the unsavoury beast slouched off with hunched back and drooping quarters.

Then the moon went down. It was pitch dark. We talked in whispers; and we both went to sleep. We were aroused by the sound of crunching bones, but we could see nothing. We had no electric appliances such as are now used to cast a flashlight upon the scene. Undoubtedly the tigress was there, and we hoped she would remain till dawn and offer a shot, but she went off while it was still quite dark. Soon after daylight our men came and we got down from our posts. The tigress had eaten a good portion of the kill during the night, and had gone off to some distant lair to which we could not track her through the intricacies of that great forest. Robert told me how, before my return to India, he sat up for a panther over a kill. It was bright moonlight, but an eclipse came on: he was tired and went to sleep. He did not wake until morning, and then found that the panther had been and had a good feed while he was sleeping peacefully in the tree above.

We returned to camp, and after breakfast went out to look at picketed buffaloes, dividing into two parties, the Subadar and Bhima accompanying me to the most distant place, where the calf had been kille. and dragged into a patch of grass and bush jungle. On our return to camp we found the other party there with news of a kill by a big tiger in the watercourse that crossed the road where the last tigress was shot. We beat this place first, and no sooner had the beaters entered the cover than the tiger roared loudly on the bank of the nullah not far from me. He had come upon a native's shoulder-cloth hung on a bush to serve as a stop, there not being enough reliable men for the purpose. He roared and rushed at the cloth, striking at it and tearing it down with his claws; he went on and roared at a stop in a tree, the man, who was a sepoy of my party, shouting back at him. Then the tiger turned back into the ravine, looking very evilly inclined, and descended the bank some thirty yards from me. I put a bullet an inch or two behind his shoulder, and, uttering no sound, he rushed up the opposite bank, where for some time he raged about in the dense cover, as though seeking someone he might slay. Soon he was quiet, I got down and went to the edge of a patch of long elephant grass into which the beast had gone. I heard no sound, and it was some time before I could distinguish the dead tiger, so closely did his coloration blend with the dry yellow grass where he lay. This beat over, we went on to the more distant kill, but the tiger could not be found.

We now went some miles down the watercourse to beat for the tiger which had killed the other buffalo. There is no need to describe the beat; it was carried out in the usual manner, and there must be some monotony in the details of the killing of every tiger. But many of these hunts present features peculiar to themselves, although it was long ago written that " one tiger dies for all." But as each tiger often possesses individual characteristics, so generally each hunt has its special features and the incidents attending the death of many tigers present considerable variation. At the usual conclave after dinner that night I remarked on the invisibility of the dead tiger in the elephant grass, which supported the theory of protective or obliterative coloration, a subject we had previously discussed at some length. The surroundings certainly concealed the tiger in a remarkable manner, but he would have been visible at once when moving.

With great regret we decided to leave the Raja's domain next day, although reluctant to abandon the chase of the tigress that had eluded us; but we did not wish to sacrifice more buffaloes on the chance of bringing to bag so cunning and elusive a beast. We were surprised to find that the Gonds in this part of the country were not very good trackers. These are indeed not so common as might be expected among the inhabitants of wild districts.

THE HUNTERS' CAMP.
On all sides resound the voices of the forest.

SMALL GAME.

TROPHIES OF THE CHASE.

At daybreak we left the shore of the great lake on which our camp had been pitched for many days and set out on our journey. A vast tract of unknown country was ahead and we had already sent on Bhima with a party to prospect. We marched twenty-eight miles that day, climbing at first by a mountain path up the steep ascent, and emerging on to a great plateau containing many small hamlets surrounded by cultivation. Our first camp was near a village owned by one whom the Raja called his brother, but in appearance this humble chief bore no resemblance to my friend who has been described. He was working in the fields with the Gond peasants, from whom he appeared to differ in no respect.

Another march of twenty miles brought us to the eastern edge of the plateau, from whence we descended into the valley below. But we were unable to take with us our carts and camels owing to the impracticability of the path, and they had to be sent with the heavy baggage by a circuitous route to a distant spot where our camp was eventually to be pitched. For the immediate present we travelled with bare necessities, our light baggage being carried down the mountain path by men from a neighbouring village. The plateau we had crossed contained little game; we saw nothing larger than a gazelle, and a hare was shot close to camp.

We had news of several tigers inhabiting the valley we now looked upon from the height, and to which we were guided by Bhima who awaited us at the head of the vale below. We descended by a steep and rugged path leading through a deep and rocky ravine; on either side rose lofty cliffs from which huge fragments of rock had been torn by wind and weather and hurled into the ravine below, causing obstructions that made the way difficult for our ponies. This narrow and secluded glen opened into a valley of little width at first, but gradually broadened out into an expanse with wooded hills on either side. A watercourse, flowing down from the ravine we had descended, contained a pebbly brook winding tortuously between verdant banks clothed with trees and shrubs, amid which the Flame of the Forest splashed its scarlet tongues, and plumes of the tamarisk filled many hollows upon the margin. Here was a welcome animation after the gloomy glen just traversed, where no living thing was to be seen, and no sound of life save the monotonous screech of cicadas struck upon the ear. But now bright peacocks glittered in the sunlight and monkeys grey and brown swung and chattered in the trees above. Ever and anon a crashing noise in the thickets announced the presence of some larger beast, alarmed by the intruders in these almost untrodden solitudes.

Our small camp, consisting of only one tent, was pitched in a dense and extensive forest close to a Gond hamlet of daub and wattle, containing no more than a dozen or so men of the same tribe as those of the country we had left behind. In exploring this wild and intricate jungle we found tracks of a family party of three, a tigress and two cubs nearly as big as herself, while, before our arrival, Bhima had already discovered the presence in this neighbourhood of at least two other tigers. But so far there was no kill, although he had picketed several buffaloes near the dry bed of the watercourse where there was ample cover of tamarisk and jamun, or wild plum. In the afternoon Robert and I fished in a pool in the stream and caught a few small chilwa, resembling the English bleak, as well as an ugly, big-headed, toad-like fish with long whiskers and spiky fins, which uttered or made in some way a peculiar noise when drawn from the water. In the evening a thunderstorm came on and drenched the forest; after dark spotted deer and peafowl calling on the banks of the watercourse gave notice that beasts of prey were on the move. There was no kill that night; the tigers appeared to have dispersed over the country, the weather being cool and water plentiful everywhere so that they could travel far and wide in search of prey. At any rate we could find no fresh tracks. There was another thunderstorm this day, and in the evening clouds again gathered. The moon was visible at fitful intervals through the black clouds that massed above; in the distance, far away, flashes of lightning proclaimed thunderstorms in more than one direction, but no rain fell in camp although the air was cooled by distant moisture. The storm was cyclonic, clinging to the encircling mountains. Later in the night the sky cleared; we were able to carry our beds out and sleep again under the stars as was our custom; by morning there was scarcely a cloud to be seen; it was pleasantly cool, a gentle breeze blew, while at times a strong gust of wind tore down the valley.

However, some of the tigers had returned from their wanderings. A kill had taken place about three miles off in a strip of jungle on a peninsula formed by an almost dry watercourse which branched at this point. We beat towards the head of the peninsula, Robert being posted in the middle on a rocky eminence while I sat on the top of the steep bank commanding a view of most of the approaches. The beat had been some time in progress when a tigress trotted across in front of me about eighty yards off, but I did not fire as she was going straight towards Robert. I was expecting to hear a shot, but as this did not happen I rightly concluded that the tigress had passed by through cover without showing herself again. Another tiger trotted across in front of me and followed almost on the same line; I shot him dead with a bullet through the heart. Then a tigress came down the nullah below me; I hit her in the middle of the back, inflicting a flesh wound, and she charged straight up the slope towards me, uttering gruff roars. When she was half-way up I killed her with a bullet that entered the neck and came out just under the skin of the right haunch whereupon she subsided without a sound. These were two well-grown cubs, each just under eight feet long. The mother tigress had escaped, passing unseen through bushes in a hollow concealed by the bank of the nullah.

We returned to camp late in the afternoon, for although the story of a beat for tigers does not take long to relate, it is a long process occupying many hours from beginning to end. In the evening a panther came prowling round the camp, uttering its harsh call at intervals. It was only to be expected that our conversation as usual turned upon the habits of animals, and we wondered how the panther could expect to find any prey when it was prowling so noisily. It seems probable that these and other felidæ hunt silently when seeking their prey. The tiger is generally a silent animal, far more so than the lion, while a famous African hunter has said that when lions roar it is a sure sign that they have already dined. We had not heard a tiger roar during this expedition except when angry or frightened or hit by a bullet, and in the latter case I observed that if a tiger utters no sound when wounded, the wound is usually quickly mortal.

Next day we found that there had been a kill on the side of the valley opposite the scene of the death of the two tigers, where the steep hillside was covered with a thick growth of bamboo jungle. This was not unexpected, for during the night we heard the roaring of the beasts quarrelling over their prey. It was a difficult beat, the ground having no pronounced features, such as lines of cover or channels and nullahs, to determine the probable direction the tigers would take, although it was obvious that it would be best to beat down towards the main watercourse. We were posted to cover a wide front, Robert being nearest the bank of the watercourse. A tiger and a tigress soon made their appearance, crossing my front at a considerable distance, and at first I had only an occasional glimpse of them between the bamboo clumps. The chance of a successful shot was very uncertain, and they were taking the direction of Robert's post so I left them alone.

Soon I heard the report of his rifle, followed by a roar, and a moment afterwards the tiger came back, moving quickly through the bamboo jungle in front of me about fifty yards off. The beaters were approaching down the hill and, hearing their shouts, the tiger stopped and executed a kind of war dance with all four feet off the ground at once, growling and dancing with rage. I shot him behind the shoulder, and he dashed off towards the beaters, uttering no sound; then he crashed into a bamboo clump, and I concluded that he was dead. I got down at once from the higher ground where I was standing behind the bamboos, followed on the trail, and found him lying dead against the clump where he had collapsed. I hoped that Robert had killed the tigress, but he had missed a very difficult shot as she made for the dense tamarisk jungle in the watercourse below, where she disappeared.

There were two kills that night by the two tigresses that had eluded us, but both beats next day were unsuccessful. One animal had eaten her fill and then gone off to a distance where it was hopeless to look for her in so extensive a forest. The other, probably the one Robert had missed, killed a buffalo calf in the thick tamarisk jungle into which she had plunged when last seen, but she was wary and no doubt angry after being hunted and losing her mate the day before. She lay still until the line approached within twenty yards or so of her lair, and then broke back with a rush and a roar, scattering the beaters in every direction. She passed very near some of the men and it was fortunate that no one was injured.

Leaving these tigresses to breed more of their kind, we marched sixteen miles to a large village where we found our heavy baggage, the weightiest item consisting of skins and other trophies, for we had with us only small tents and the scantiest camp furniture. Here were many tigers within a ten mile radius, and four or five were brought to bag within a week. In this jungle a few years before a Rohilla shikari was killed by a wounded tiger; the people were told not to go near the spot as the beast was still alive, but the shikari went up to it before he could be stopped and the frightful wounds he sustained were fatal the same night. Here also a report reached us that a man-eating tiger had created a reign of terror, being in the habit of lying near a roadside shrine and taking men from passing carts; it was said that the people were afraid to venture out except in large parties. We rode over to the place next morning, but could find no grounds for the report except a tradition of some years back, although there was by the side of the road a heap of stones formed by those passers-by who, in accordance with custom, had flung each one à stone upon the spot where a man had been killed by a tiger. This rumour was typical of many such jungle tales; these are generally exaggerated and have a tendency to persist and be brought up to date with picturesque additions, even when founded on fact. Often they have no basis of truth, for travellers' tales are not the only doubtful ones.

CHAPTER XVIII

TRACKS OF DEATH

AFTER several long marches, we had at length reached the last encampment on the edge of the tiger country. We would then emerge on to the open plain, stretching as far as the old cantonment, where the country consisted mainly of cultivation, broken at times by ranges of low bush-clad hills or patches of jungle holding a few panthers and bears but not wild and secluded enough for tigers. The panther, as will be seen, sometimes lives almost within the precincts of a village and constantly haunts the hills, valleys, and ravines in the neighbourhood of human habitations, where he can prowl round the hamlets at night and pick up stray dogs, calves, or goats, or perhaps a child that has been left to itself by careless parents.

Our tents stood on the bank of a watercourse that in the rainy season would no doubt have been a considerable river, but was now almost destitute of water. Although we had met with so many storms, and had been so often flooded with rain during our wanderings, this part of the country was now quite dry throughout. It was on the north side of a range of hills crossed by a narrow and precipitous pass, this watershed forming a line of demarcation between the wet and the dry country.

When we arrived in camp after a long morning's ride, mostly through forest, we found that the people had been terrorised by a man-eating panther which haunted the neighbourhood. The beast had, however, been destroyed some time before, although in the usual manner in these wilds its existence had been extended by rumour to the present time. However, all was now well; the peasants were occupied with their usual pursuits, and were at night no longer sleeping in terror but in security on the thresholds of their huts. Still many had piteous tales to tell. The village grain-dealer, who attended our camp with supplies for man and beast, had himself lost a young son who had been devoured by this monster. The child, a boy about nine years old, was taken from the bed in which he was sleeping beside his father in front of the house in the open air, for the nights were very hot. The man felt the sheet pulled off and woke up, and the boy was gone. The night was dark, and although the track of blood was followed for some distance by the light of lanterns, these were soon lost in the dense thicket to which they led. In the morning they found the blood-stained loin cloth, and farther on the hands and feet of the child.

After leaving the great tiger jungles, we moved across a tract of cultivated country where empty and uncultivated fields, burnt brick-red by the scorching summer sun, bore sad testimony to the tracks of famine and of death. We came to a considerable watercourse containing not a drop of water. At one spot a veritable Golgotha of human skulls and other bones lay near what had been a water-hole excavated in the shingle and sand of the empty river-bed, sad emblems of famine and death in this lonely spot where poor human creatures had gasped out their lives, the bones gnawed and scattered by foul birds and beasts. So also the traces of starvation and disease were evident on the roadsides and on the outskirts of villages where the dead had been hastily buried in shallow graves, from which the remains had been torn by jackals and dogs, so even after life had gone they could not rest quietly in their graves.

And if so many evidences of the tracks of death in a few short marches were clearly present in the light of day, what ghastly tragedies must have been enacted in the more hidden spots and in jungles to which many poor creatures wandered in search of sustenance, only to fall victims to starvation and disease. It has been suggested that tigers have acquired a predilection for human flesh from their finding prey among the dead and dying victims of years of scarcity. I have remarked that man-eating tigers were uncommon in the part of the country we had so far traversed, but we now entered a district where there was a tradition of man-eating dating back at least to the middle of the nineteenth century. It is indeed remarkable how these abnormal individuals of their species persist in particular localities. Thus when there were tigers in the neighbourhood of Bombay, many were man-eaters. The same may be said of the man-eaters of Bengal, particularly of the Sundarbans of the Ganges delta, these islands having a very bad reputation, especially since two Europeans were killed there at the end of the eighteenth century. Portions of the Central Provinces also have always been infamous for the prevalence of tigers and other carnivora preying on human beings.

The traditional man-eater is a decrepit, old, and sometimes mangy beast, perhaps incapacitated by wounds which have made it difficult for it to kill ordinary prey. Certainly this is sometimes the case, but on the other hand a man-eating tiger or leopard may be a vigorous animal in the prime of life, while a mangy condition has certainly nothing to do with the eating of human flesh, which is as nourishing as any other. More often man-eating is an acquired and surely never an inherited attribute; it appears to be commoner among the female than the male sex. This is susceptible of explanation, as is the prevalence of the habit in particular districts. A tigress hard put to it to find enough wild or domesticated animals for the satisfaction of her own hunger and that of her offspring may well take to preying on human victims as an easier quarry. The most probable explanation of the continuance of the habit in particular districts is that the young, being thus fed on human flesh, and perhaps being taught to seize and kill people, acquire the habit and in their turn pass it on to their companions and their descendants. It is thus perpetuated unless the whole brood addicted to man-eating is destroyed.

We encamped at a spot where Robert had missed a panther the previous year. This animal inhabited a long, narrow, and wooded watercourse and an easy shot was missed in an unaccountable manner. Just after the panther came a swarm of bees, fortunately of the smaller species, which had been disturbed by the beaters, and all had to run for their lives. Robert had a few stings in the back of his head, and would have suffered much more severely but for the devotion of Chandru and Nathu who, he afterwards found, had voluntarily sacrificed themselves by keeping behind him, thus intercepting the larger part of the swarm and attracting the bees to themselves. Chandru was very severely stung, his neck being covered in parts with patches of stings so thickly set that they looked like brown fur. It took some hours to extract all the stings.

We went out a few miles after small game, having first sent off the carts with baggage to the next camping ground, not expecting to meet with anything larger than a hare or a peafowl, so the rifles went with the camp. Then we met a goatherd who said he had seen a panther lying under a bush a couple of miles off. Fortunately I had a buckshot cartridge in my pocket. With a dozen beaters we climbed over some rocky hills to the spot, guided by the herdsman, not far from the scene of the previous adventure with the bees, where the panther lay in a broad valley with scattered bush. Placing a man as marker on each side of the valley, we sent the rest to beat through the jungle while we squatted behind a bush. Soon after the beat began a frantic yelling on one side of the valley announced that the game was afoot and had tried to break out, but had been driven back. And then suddenly the panther appeared from behind a bush close to me. He saw me as I raised my gun and his face broke into a snarling grin; I fired on the instant, and expected to see the beast coming through the smoke, so had my finger on the trigger of the other barrel, loaded only with a charge of small shot. But the buckshot was unexpectedly effective, and when the smoke cleared I saw the panther, shot through behind the shoulder at eighteen yards' distance, struggling in its death throes. We enquired whether this panther had done any harm in the neighbourhood; the headman of a village said that a child had been carried off by some animal some six months ago, and that they had found only a few bones and the hands and feet, but he could not say whether this was the culprit or not.

At our next encampment we once more reached some heavy and more extensive jungle. Our tents were pitched in a grove of mango trees much frequented by bears from adjacent rocky hills when the fruit was ripe, while the neighbourhood was formerly notorious for its man-eating tigers and panthers. Rumours of the presence of a man-eating tiger had reached us, the number of its victims being put at ten or twelve. Only a few days before a Banjara tending cattle had been carried off and devoured, the monster leaving, as is common with all man-eaters, the head, hands, and feet of the victim. It did not, however, confine its depredations to human beings, as that night a buffalo was killed by a tiger about a mile from our camp, and undoubtedly the culprit was the man-eater, for its tracks were known to the village shikaris who said no other tiger frequented that part of the jungle.

Robert was posted at the head of the ravine in which the kill had taken place, while I sat on the top of the fairly steep slope a couple of hundred yards farther back. Soon after the beat began, a terrific roaring in the bush cover below announced both the presence and the anger of the monster. He attempted to break out on the far side of the ravine, but the yells of the beaters on that flank drove him back into dense bush below me, and then the beaters were confused in the intricate cover, not knowing which way to go amid all the uproar and the shouting. The tiger remained some ten minutes in the thicket into which he had retreated, and was there beset and hemmed in, and as men crowded round the cover I was afraid that some would be injured, for before long the frightened and infuriated tiger must certainly break through them; something must inevitably give way. I went some distance down the hillside, partly in the vain hope of getting a sight and possibly a shot, although that was not likely in such cover and would scarcely be safe amid such a crowd, and partly to clear a way for the tiger to find a way out, like the " golden bridge " we have (I am inclined to think wrongly) been advised in savage warfare to leave for the escape of the enemy. Soon I managed to clear my side of the thicket and leave it open while the beaters on the far side were instructed to raise a further uproar. I scrambled up my hillside, and reached the frail but friendly shelter of a great ant-hill at the top, just as the tiger burst through the koranda bush below me and galloped up the slope, growling fiercely, with every hair and whisker set as he came. I shot him through the body and put in two or three more bullets as he scrambled about and still showed signs of life. In fact, it was advisable to shoot until he was dead, for some beaters were still wandering about not far off although most of them had climbed into the trees. This was a fine tiger in the prime of life, with teeth in perfect condition and coat of a dark burnt sienna colour, so there was no apparent reason for his taking to man-eating. But perhaps he was a descendant of the man-eaters of long ago to whom their evil propensities had come down.

The habit of man-eaters of leaving the extremities of their human victims, just as the dogs left of Jezebel only " the skull and the feet and the palms of her hands," has often been referred to and is a matter of common observation. So the famous Chithu, the Pindari chieftain, who, wandering alone in the jungle on the banks of the Tapti River after the defeat and dispersal of his robber horde in 1818, fell a victim to a man-eating tiger, his remains being identified by the discovery of his head and a satchel containing his papers in the monster's lair. Not long ago similar relics were observed, left by wolves which killed a man near Constantinople, the incident giving rise to some correspondence in the Press as to the reason for such rejections of the feet in particular in the case of human victims. But the explanations offered were more ingenious than well-founded.

It was suggested by one writer that, owing to the soles of the feet of people accustomed to going barefooted being covered with a thick and tough cuticle, the man-eater finds them unpalatable. But surely animals able to masticate the tough hides of oxen and other wild and domesticated beasts would have no difficulty in chewing and swallowing the skin on the sole of a man's foot, however tough. Moreover, such a theory is only a partial explanation, and does not account for the rejection of the skull and the hands, nor would it explain why the same members of children of tender years and tender skins are similarly treated, the little hands with yellow palms upturned as if to call on heaven for mercy and for vengeance, as I have myself seen them. Certainly there have been exceptions as in the case of a twelve-year-old boy, whose dismembered body was found in the fork of a tree where a leopard had placed it, while three fingers were disinterred from the beast's stomach after it was shot.

As for Jezebel, the hands and the face may have been tainted even to the taste of dogs by unpalatable cosmetics; but the soles of her feet were not likely to be covered by a thick cuticle, for it is improbable that a lady of her condition would have walked unshod, if she ever walked at all. It seems clear that these extremities are rejected owing to the man-eater not having the sense to distinguish between the hands and feet of the human being and the four hoofs of its ordinary prey. Similarly, the head of a man would appear to the beast as uneatable as the head, sometimes horned and always hard and bony, of an ox, a deer, an antelope, or a hog. This inability to distinguish such differences is not confined to wild beasts, unless we include in that category the Papuan cannibals who cooked a white man in his boots and tried to eat them, thinking they were a part of the feet of a human being who was strange to them.

We were yet to come upon more tracks of death, not only in the marks of famine on our journey back to the cantonment from this spot, but in stories of the deeds of thugs, some of whom still lingered in the gaol where they had been confined on the discovery and extermination or dispersal of their gangs, and had lived to great old age in the prison. Thugs were both Hindus and Mohammedans, bound together by curious religious ceremonies connected with the goddess Bhowani. They strangled their victims with a large cloth or kerchief, called a *rumal*, having a slip knot and knotted at the end to facilitate holding. This cloth on a given signal was skilfully cast round the victim's neck and the strangling done in a few moments with the greatest force and the tightest grip of skilful and experienced hands.

Not far from our way there had passed on his travels and been tracked to his death a noble Moslem soldier who had fought on many a field, but fell a victim to a thug as described by Colonel Meadows Taylor. The thug in his confession related how he had thrown the strangling cloth about this nobleman's neck and " the Nawab snored several times like a man in a deep sleep, but my grip was firm and did not relax—a horse would have died under it. Suddenly, as he writhed under me, every muscle in his body quivered ; he snored again still louder, and the now yielding form offered no resistance. I gazed upon his features, and saw that the breath of life had passed from the body it had but now animated. Subzee Khan was dead—I had destroyed the slayer of hundreds ! " And so at last Death had tracked down the mighty warrior !

INDEX

A

Abdul, 22
Acacia, 17, 33, 93
Africa, 52, 54, 60, 63, 66
Ahmednagar, 87
Alcock, 68
Alligator, 71
Alta Velo, 56
Ambari, 174 et seq., 194
Anicut, 18, 223
Antelope, 19, 35, 73, 80, 88, 98, 104, 115, 125, 136, 148, 174, 207
Apa Sahib, 83
Aristotle, 145
Augusta, Fort, 59
Ayah, 21, 26
Azores, 57

B

Bandit, 75
Banjara, 90 et seq., 157, 175, 186, 195, 245
Banyan, 17, 24, 30, 94, 99, 102, 193
Barbados, 46, 66 et seq.
Barbet, 102, 109
Bat, 99
Bathing, 49
Bear, 19, 43, 76, 100, 126, 131, 135, 150, 158 et seq., 174, 186, 194, 198
Beata, Cape, 56
Bees, 113, 243

Bhil, 108, 186
Bhima, 108, 115, 119 et seq., 135, 139, 140, 151, 157, 164, 170, 178 et seq., 184, 196 et seq., 231, 233
Bhowani, 248
Bijli, 27, 30
Bikanir, 115
Bison, 19, 43, 77, 81, 127, 148, 169, 176, 219
Blackbuck, 26, 27, 28, 98
Blue Mountains, 59, 66
Boar, 142, 151, 172
Bridgetown, 67, 68
Buckshot, 154, 244
Buddha, 82, 126, 161
Buffalo, 34, 95, 108, 113 et seq., 135, 146, 157, 168, 178 et seq.
Bulbul, 20, 35, 194
Bush, Colonel, 61
Bustard, 27, 35, 83, 89, 98

C

Camel, 27, 31, 96, 103, 107
Cape Beata, 56
Caribbean Sea, 46, 58
Caribs, 58
Carissima, 21
Carlisle Bay, 67
Ceylon, 160
Chandru, 108, 120, 124, 128, 135, 145, 157, 172, 184, 194, 196, 206 243
Chase Colonel, 69
Cheetah, 83, 118

Chichkora, 108, 124 et seq., 135, 139 et seq.
Christchurch, 69
Cicada, 103, 133
Clavicles, 129
Columbus, 56, 58
Combermere, 60
Constantinople, 247
Coral, 70
Cornwallis, 59
Craven, Corporal, 61
Crocodile, 138, 164 et seq., 221, 224
Crows, 43, 51, 65, 94

D

Daaga, 60, 61
Deer, 19, 77, 80, 81, 102, 115, 125, 135, 137, 148, 171, 207, 229
Deo, 126
Dog, wild, 79, 167, 176, 194
Dominica, 60, 61
Dove, 20, 43, 194
Ducks, 19, 63, 83, 208, 221
Duppies, 70

E

Elephant, 19, 23, 77, 133
Enteric fever, 64, 68
Execution, military, 61

F

Falcon, 38
Famine, 86 et seq., 105, 106, 241 et seq.
"Far Away," 66
Flame of the forest, 151
Flowerpecker, 37

Flycatchers, 20, 109, 191
Flying fox, 24
Fort, 82, 103, 222
Fort Augusta, 58
Fox, 35, 88
Francolin, 25, 28, 35, 147
French master, 54

G

Ganges, 178, 217, 242
Gautama, 161
Gazelle, 27, 73, 83, 88, 98, 114, 148, 171, 233
Ghost story, 67
God, jungle, 127, 181, 216
Gold Mohur tree, 151
Gond, 82, 127, 175, 186, 212 et seq.
Green pigeon, 20, 28, 99
Guadaloupe, 60
Guineafowl, 63

H

Haiti, 57, 58, 66
Hare, 35, 83, 91, 207, 233
Hastings rocks, 46
Himalaya, 118, 121
Hindu, 127, 148, 214, 217, 224, 248
Hislop, Sir T., 97
Hispaniola, 56 et seq.
Hornet, 113
Hyena, 26, 35, 107, 126, 154, 230

I

Immolation, 217
Indru, 220
Invalides, 54

INDEX

J

Jabalpur, 113
Jackal, 24, 35, 98, 105, 133, 153, 178, 183
Jackdaw, 43, 51
Jacmel, 66
Jamaica, 46, 56, 59, 64, 66, 68
Jane Ann, 67
Jay, 38, 43
Jezebel, 246
Jhansi, 98

K

Kali, the destroyer, 127, 217
Kestrel, 43, 51
Kingston, 59, 62
Kite, 35
Koel, 20, 194
Korkus, 217, 219
Krishna, 213

L

Lakshmi, 19, 23
Langur, 102
Lemnos, 45
Leopard, 20, 43, 100, 104, 112, 117

M

Mahadeo, 83
Malaya, 178
Mandhata, 217, 218
Man-eater, 113, 117, 224, 241 et seq.
Mango, 17, 30, 95
Maratha, 97, 100, 158, 193, 217
Marble Rocks, 113
Marlowe, 145

Martinique, 59
McPherson, 65
Mehidpur, 97
Merry, Sergeant, 61
Mohenjo Daru, 160
Mohwa, 81, 148
Mongoose, 63, 230
Monkey, 81, 94, 102, 133, 146, 176, 230, 233
Morgan, Sir Henry, 62
Moslem, 22, 97, 111, 149, 152, 188, 217, 222, 248
Moth, 43
Mudros, 45
Muktagiri, 82
Mullet, 70
Murder, 68
Mysore, 158, 207

N

Nagpur, 83, 102
Napoleon, 54, 60
Narbada, 99, 101, 113, 217
Nathu, 22, 26, 30, 108, 120, 124, 128, 135, 143, 155, 161, 182, 193, 203, 224, 243
Nightingale, Colonel, 190
Nile, 44
Nilgai, 80, 108, 136, 142, 148, 176

O

Omkar, 218
Oriole, 36, 109
Owl, 20, 43, 64, 194

P

Palisadoes, 46, 59, 62
Palm, 17

INDEX

Panama, 62
Pangolin, 210
Panther, 19, 29, 79, 81, 91, 108, 116, 122, 132, 152, 164, 172 et seq., 203, 240 et seq.
Paroquet, 87, 95, 109
Parsis, 89
Partridge, 25, 35, 84, 88, 98, 207
Peafowl, 76, 98, 102, 109, 121, 133, 147, 233
Persian wheel, 29
Pigeon, 20, 28, 43, 64, 103, 113, 194
Pindari, 18, 35, 99, 101, 217, 246
Pipal, 17, 30
Plague, Corporal, 61
Pliny, 145
Pogson, Ensign, 61
Poker, 74
Porcupine, 78, 88, 126, 144
Port au Prince, 58
Porto Rico, 57
Port Royal, 59, 62, 65
Prophet, the, 111, 114
Pyre, 218

Q

Quail, 84, 88, 207

R

rájá, 221 et seq.
Rajput, 101
Rajputana, 115
Regiment, 22, 30, 41, 55, 59, 62
Robert, 40, 50, 55, 94, 105, 122, 135 et seq., 148 et seq., 171 et seq., 180 et seq., 200 et seq., 236 et seq.
Rose, Sir Hugh, 98

S

St. Lucia, 61
St. Thomas Island, 57
Sambar, 77, 80, 115, 133, 148, 175, 194
Sandgrouse, 27, 84
San Domingo, 57
Satpuras, 217
Saugor, 98
Sea wolves, 56, 57
Sehore, 98
Shaikh Farid, 26, 108, 111, 125, 139 et seq., 192
Shaikh Karim, 94, 106, 114, 121, 141
Sharks, 64
Shikari, 115, 123, 142, 146, 151, 157, 177, 207, 222, 228
Sikh, 166, 175, 186
Singapore, 178
Singarwari, 193
Skeleton, 223
Snakes, 79, 94, 100, 113, 198, 206
Snipe, 63, 83, 88
Sombrero, 57
Spanish, 56, 62, 63
Spirit of the Wild, 111, 127, 181, 190
Squirrel, 20, 37, 64, 94, 104
Stag, 126, 131, 137, 161, 175, 229
Subadar, 97, 105, 111 et seq., 121 et seq., 135, 152 et seq., 172 et seq., 184 et seq., 195, 204, 211, 222, 231
Sundarbans, 178, 242
Sundial, 37

T

Tamarind, 17
Tamarisk, 233, 238
Tapti, 213, 217, 246
Taylor, Meadows, 99, 248
Telinga, 186
Thugs, 19, 99, 102, 248

INDEX

Thunderstorm, 178, 235
Tiger, 19 *et seq.*, 43, 74 *et seq.*, 104 *et seq.*, 138 *et seq.*, 160 *et seq.*, 177 *et seq.*, 196 *et seq.*, 227 *et seq.*
Tortuga, 58
Tower of Silence, 89
Trinidad, 60, 71
Trout, 39, 50
Turks Island, 64
Turtle, 165

U

Umarkhed, 102
Up Park Camp, 59, 64 *et seq.*

V

Valhalla, 32
Victorian Age, 52 *et seq.*
Voodoo, 58
Vultures, 35, 79, 100, 105, 120, 137, 163, 183

W

Wapping, 62
Water ouzel, 43
Wazir Khan, 22, 26, 31
Wellington, 87, 97, 100, 118, 158
West India Regiment, 62 *et seq.*
West Indies, 55 *et seq.*
Wild dog, 79, 80, 176, 194
Wolf, 20, 35, 98, 168
Woodpecker, 38, 43

Y

Yakub Khan, 22, 24, 26, 31
Yellow Jack, 62, 64, 66, 67

Z

Zambesi, 44
Ziarat, 111